POWER OF W

Praise for *Power of W*

'The author has deeply been on an inner consciousness journey for a considerable amount of time and her realisations – psychological, social, and spiritual – are gifts to the potential readers of the book. I particularly enjoyed her use of acronyms throughout the book. Her primary focus is on women becoming consciously present to the fullness of their femininity and masculinity and their abiding, divine presence, realisations that are also critical for men.

Indeed, even though the book is primarily directed at women, particularly those in the second half of life – I certainly would recommend these women to read the book – but I would also recommend men in the second half of life to read it too. If women deserve to come into the fullness of their femininity, masculinity and divinity, so too do men.

Her quotation from Dalai Rumi that "the depth of our suffering can result in the height of our own joy" beautifully captures the author's intentions in drafting this book.'

Dr Tony Humphreys, consultant clinical psychologist and course director, University College Cork and Technological University of the Shannon

'*Power of W* is an invitation to explore our authentic selves as we move towards and through the aging process and into the Third Act of our lives. Ann brings a wealth of experience from her own personal and professional journey. Her exploration of this transition is woven into steps we can all use to reflect on and explore this journey for ourselves. She writes about moving truthfully and passionately into the fullness of our selves as she challenges us to rethink our world view of aging, sexuality and all our relationships from lovers to children, grandchildren, friends and those in our communities. In doing this, she stretches the parameters of our well-worn habits and invites us to expand into exploration and discussion on such topics as sex after 50, feelings of failure in relationship, internalized misogyny, the ancient wisdom of our druidic and Celtic ancestors, consciousness, morality and death. Throughout, she urges us to remember the centrality of our spiritual nature. Her writing emphasises the necessity of making space for deepening our self-awareness and holds strong the value of blossoming into and enjoying this time in our lives while also making valuable contributions from a place of earned wisdom. Expanding our consciousness fruitfully, she urges, is core to improve and underpin positive and proactive growth and change in our lives. This personal and collective invitation poses interesting and intriguing questions that invite us to reflect and think about our individual and collective journey. This is done through story, inquiry and experiential exercises which both challenge and support us to open our thinking and our hearts to ourselves and each other. Ann's book is a great read and a useful guide to awakening the truth of our potential and powerfully supports our evolution into elderhood, wisdom and legacy.'

Anne Gaffney, biodynamic and integrative psychotherapist, trainer and supervisor

'This book was a joy to read. The concept of our Third Act as women is so important, and is very beautifully and thoughtfully laid out for our understanding by Ann. The raw honesty in the book gives it depth, and encouraged me to personally reflect on my own journey into the future. The importance of 'our Authentic selves' and making our voices heard is softly highlighted, and the pathways and suggestions that are suggested will benefit so many women as they move into this wonderful 'Third Act'. I appreciated the sense of strength, honest advice, and guidance. I really enjoyed *Power of W: Women Thriving in Their Third Act*; I believe it will be a book I return to many times as I prepare for my own Third Act.'

Margaret Cox, director ICE Group and Pitman Training

'In her book, *Power of W: Women Thriving in Their Third Act*, author Ann McGarry makes a strong case for the incredible richness and satisfaction awaiting women who are willing to do the work involved to develop their authentic selves. Her discovery to "stop doing anything that did not make me feel good", is inspirational for women as they journey through their lives. The opportunity to use her prompts in workbook form further urges women forward. A treasure for women of any age as they anticipate a long and fulfilling life.'

Joanne B. Sullivan, Assistant Vice President of Community Engagement, USF Health/University of South Florida

'*Power of W* by Ann McGarry is a must-read for anyone who wants to plan a retirement that is energising and purposeful, and not just full of activity for activity's sake. Ann invites the reader to work through the 3 Cs (Conscious presence, Connection and Contribution) to discover their true selves and to step up and claim centre stage in the Third Act. Starting with a reflection on where you are now and exploring topics such as relationships, mortality and quest for purpose, this book will resonate with anyone at this stage of life. A wonderful blend of spirituality and reflection, but with practical questions to prompt action and goal-setting. Sharing the personal application of the 3 Cs towards the end is useful and also affirms and validates the power of this self-development model. A timely read for me which has reframed some of my anxieties about the next phase in my life – this Divine Feminine has been awakened!'

Josephine Walsh, career coach, trainer, facilitator and Head of Career Development Centre, University of Galway

'*Power of W* is an engaging and inspirational read that aids readers to find and foster their inner voice and divine feminine power – a power that when harnessed and nurtured will allow you to tap into the true essence of who you are and your offering to the world you both reside in and are part of.'

Greg Muller, leadership and human performance coach, www.leadthepack.net

Power of W

Women Thriving in Their Third Act

Ann McGarry

Orpen Press

Published by
Orpen Press
Upper Floor, Unit B3
Hume Centre, Hume Avenue
Park West Industrial Estate
Dublin 12

email: info@orpenpress.com
www.orpenpress.com

Paperback ISBN 978-1-78605-189-9
ePub ISBN 978-1-78605-190-5

This publication is sold with the understanding that the publisher and author are not engaged in rendering psychological, financial, legal or other professional services. If expert assistance or counselling is needed, the services of a competent professional should be sought.

Printed in Dublin by SPRINTprint Ltd

To the women of my own ancestral line – O'Connor and McGarry families. To these women who went before me, thank you for your contribution and your rich legacy of adventure, courage, creativity, education, enterprise, faith, and persistent and resilient spirit.

To all women journeying to develop wholeness in their lives. To those women stepping into the defining final stage of life, the Third Act.

This book is dedicated to all women who value the wholeness of their lives. This book encourages women to live from their authentic selves, fearlessly and courageously expressing their uniqueness.

About the Author

Ann is a human development consultant, trainer and coach, supporting organisations, teams and individuals to develop and grow. Her coaching and training programmes act as a catalyst to unleash talent, thereby supporting personal fulfilment whilst also delivering organisational goals. Her training programmes include leadership, change and strategic management, management development, and wellness, and have been delivered to the public and private sectors, from SMEs to large corporations, either as open or in-house courses.

Ann McGarry has provided quality consultancy services internationally to the highly regulated pharmaceutical and medical devices sectors. Prior to setting up her consultancy practice, she held senior quality assurance roles in the pharmaceutical and allied sectors for twenty years, where staff development formed a significant part of her role.

Her lecturing experience includes the University of Limerick, NUI Galway (now known as University of Galway) and Galway–Mayo Institute of Technology (now part of Atlantic Technological University), delivering on human resource development, supervisory management, quality management and wellness topics.

Ann is a strong advocate of lifelong learning. She graduated with a B.Sc. in Chemistry from NUI Galway in 1977 and obtained additional technical qualifications – a Diploma in Industrial Management and a Certificate in Total Quality Management from Dublin Institute of Technology and Irish Management Institute, respectively. She then expanded her studies to personal development over the last 20 years to include a Certificate in Stress Reduction and Relaxation Counselling

(Stress Management Institute of Ireland), a Diploma in Training and Development (Irish Institute of Training and Development), a Certificate in Neuro-Linguistic Programming (Society of NLP) and a Diploma in Professional Coaching (Irish Coach Institute). In 2012 she graduated with an M.Sc. in Work and Organisational Behaviour from University of Limerick, with her thesis centring on the development of leadership effectiveness.

Her passion for the development of human potential and capacities inspired her to write her first book, *CARE of Leadership: A Practice for Developing Leadership Effectiveness* (Orpen Press, 2017).

Her more recent focus has been directed to the 'Third Act' and living life to the highest potential: as she describes it, living more from the Authentic Self. This calling has resulted in the publication of her second book, *Power of W: Women Thriving in Their Third Act*. Her latest training programme, 'REIGNITE: The Retirement Ready Programme', echoes the theme of living a meaningful and fulfilling Third Act.

She lives between Ireland and Portugal, pursuing her passion to communicate as a writer, delivering personal development programmes and painting. She regularly walks Caminos in Galicia, Spain.

Acknowledgements

In bringing *Power of W: Women Thriving in Their Third Act* from manuscript to publication it is important to recognise the significant contributions of:

Eileen O'Brien, my editor, for her invaluable support and advice throughout the editing process in getting my contribution in my Third Act to market. I also acknowledge the team at Orpen Press for their faith in my second book.

To my parents, James and Sarah (both deceased), for the gift of life and love of learning.

And finally, to my maternal grandmother for her lifelong inspiration and courage, and for guiding me to Santiago de Compostela.

Preface

Women's roles in home life, society and career have possibly never have received so much focus and attention in history as they have in recent years. Much of this focus has been dominated by career: modern women's efforts to valiantly juggle family life while not compromising opportunities for career advancement and growth.

Outside the home, the place of women in society and business life is important. Their presence worldwide in these areas provides benefits, as their 'take' is that seen through the 'female lens.' This female perspective acts as complementary to their male counterparts.

In healthy organisations the female 'take' does not negate or compete with the male perspective. Rather, these organisations benefit from the enhanced differing perspectives that add a further dimension to the situation at hand. These in turn bring richness to creative processes, problem-solving and decision-making, all necessary to successfully navigate the continued challenges of an ever-changing world.

Throughout the ages in modern history, women have struggled to express and experience all the natural aspects of their humanity and be heard. The time is ripe now; never before has it been more relevant in the evolution of society for women's perspectives and contributions to be acknowledged, respected, and acted upon. Women need to continue their advancements, in expanding and deepening their confidence and commitment to follow through with making these inroads in society at large.

Women need the expression of all their natural aspects – in their family life, their career, their role in the community and, finally, their contribution, which I believe is generally seen to best effect in one's Third Act.

Retirement has become an increasingly topical subject in today's world. The reality is that people are living longer today than in previous generations. On average we are living 30+ years longer than our great-grandparents' generation. In effect, this extension is like a second adulthood life. Women tend to live longer than men and therefore make up the greater percentage of this senior population.

So, how are we going to react to the gift of these additional years?

The word 'retirement' can meet with a spectrum of responses, ranging from fear on the one hand to elation and a wonderful sense of freedom on the other.

There is a plethora of financial houses and organisations offering advice, with the predominant focus on the financial aspect of capability for retirement. Regrettably, there is a significant lack of attention paid to the non-financial side of the retirement equation, and in particular to the inner journey to make this significant transition as effective as possible.

The impetus for this book is that I believe that women can play a significant role in society. Their influence on the younger generation can be a tremendously valuable legacy. Living a passionate life, filled with joy and love in conscious awareness of our Self, may indeed be our most significant gift to future generations. Nowhere could this be more significant than in the Third Act for women in their Wise Woman's phase. This term will be developed in the chapters that follow. The Wise Woman refers to a woman who is venerated for their experience, judgement, and wisdom.

This book presents my thoughts on how women can live a more impactful life – a life that is going deeper, developing into wholeness. This life can be lived from conscious presence, connecting into your truer nature, your True Self, and reflecting this through living from your Authentic Self. This life is one where connections and relationships develop and are sustained by your best self. A life that also leaves a gift for future generations through your unique contribution. These three aspects have the greatest potential to fuse and synergise in your Third Act as you emerge a Wise Woman.

I have entered my Third Act. For me life is now about living joyfully, being present to each moment and reconnecting with Who I Really Am – a Divine Being having a human experience. It is about engaging with all aspects of my roles and connecting with community and, finally, I hope that I am making my contribution through my books, training programmes/seminars, and related projects. In all these aspects I continue to become more consciously present, embracing life, participating, and enjoying life from a loving and joyful heart.

My hope is that this book will in some way provide a stimulus and support you may need, particularly in the last phase of life, your Third Act.

Live the life of your dreams, recreate and reunite with what gives you joy and celebrate every day of your life. This is a special time for you now to reconnect and reveal more of who you really are; for your divine essence experiencing and expressing your uniqueness. Live your life from a Conscious Presence, connecting into your community and leaving your unique legacy by thriving in your Third Act.

Enjoy.

Contents

Acknowledgements .... **x**

Preface .... **xi**

Part I – Introduction to Power of W: Women Thriving in Their Third Act **1**

1. Introduction 3

2. How this Book Came to Be 8

3. Sections in the Book 10

4. Concluding Comments 12

Part II – The 3 Cs: Conscious Presence, Connection and Contribution – Essentials for Us **13**

5. Introduction 15

6. First C: Conscious Presence 19

7. Second C: Connection 48

8. Third C: Contribution 72

Part III – Ann's Story: Thoughts and Interactions with the 3 Cs 89

9. Introduction. 91

10. First C: Thoughts on Interacting with Conscious Presence 97

11. Second C: Thoughts on Interacting with Connection 110

12. Third C: Thoughts on Interacting with Contribution 114

Part IV – Concluding Comments 123

13. Final Thoughts. 125

Appendix 127

References 139

PART I

Introduction to Power of W: Women Thriving in Their Third Act

1

Introduction

Today, our lifespan is about thirty years longer than that of our great-grandparents. These additional years of life could be viewed as another full phase of adulthood. As women, on average, live longer than men it may be reasonable to state that women form a sizeable portion of this senior population. I believe these additional years can therefore present women in their Third Act with opportunities to influence society and the world – to make significant inroads to our individual and collective contributions. I feel that we really have a chance to make a difference, to leave a legacy to future generations. These years are not just about filling in this time with endless activity for activity's sake. I believe that we have been given this time for a good reason. We have an opportunity to review, to take stock of our life to date. Through this exercise we can reclaim things that were important to us in earlier years which we may have cast aside, we can reassess our values and priorities now and make necessary adjustments, we can redefine who we are, and we can reconnect with our passion and creativity. This exercise may also throw up some remorse and gives us the opportunity to make amends. Also, and this may often be overlooked, we can rejoice in and recognise our strengths and achievements. We may indeed wish to reclaim and carry these through to the next phase of our lives.

This gift that we have been given with these additional years presents us with the opportunity to develop into wholeness. A time for us to become wise and demonstrate and pass on wisdom. Finally, this time presents us with the greatest gift of all: to become, experience and live our lives from our Authentic Self. A time to live and enjoy life, giving full expression to our unique divinity – living and experiencing Who We Really Are centred in our Authentic Self.

Living from this Authentic Self and as it aligns more with our True Self, we experience life more wholly; we are more confident, dropping our anxiety and worry; we achieve more in a relaxed way; and we interact with others in more meaningful, considered, and loving ways.

It may be helpful at this point to pause and describe these terms, and also that of 'Source', which is discussed later.

Your '*Authentic Self*' means the part of you that is not defined by your roles, possessions, or expectations of others. It is your true, genuine, and natural inner essence or core identity. It is the composite of all your skills, talents, and wisdom. Being your Authentic Self means aligning your words, actions, and behaviours with who you really are deep down.

Your '*True Self*' can be called your 'higher self' or your 'soul'. It may be best to describe it in terms of the experiences with their associated feelings when connected with your True Self. Feelings include being calm, centred, free and peaceful. Deepening your connection, aligning more with your True Self brings more expansive feelings, such as: bliss, intuition, joy, loving-kindness, and empathy. The True Self is a natural state, although we need to develop a practice to sustain and abide in it more in our daily lives because of competing selves. So, by deepening our access to the True Self, the other selves tend to fall away, resulting in the longer we can abide in the state of pure consciousness. The additional feelings that accompany this are feelings of: lightness, being centred, safe, that life has meaning, the desire to serve, being *in* your life, bliss in normal, everyday activity and increase in insights. (As described by Deepak Chopra.)

Source: There are many terms used to describe 'Source'. Often referred to as 'energy', 'cosmic energy', 'universal energy field', 'pure potential', 'pure consciousness', 'the field of infinite possibilities', or 'the source of all creation'. In religious terms it is God, our Creator.

Living from this space means that we continue to grow and evolve. We are actively engaged with the higher motivational needs not only of growth for ourselves, but also of service to others and of contribution. We are on a mission to find our way back to our true home – to merge with Divine Consciousness. To realise and remember that we were always connected to it: there is no separation and there never was. It is a journey to reconnect, to remember Who We Truly Are.

In this phase we are more attuned with our inner guidance. We are clearer on our purpose and the meaning of our lives and why we are here. We have been given an opportunity to lead the way, to be an example and hold the light for future generations. We stand at the bridge between past generations and future generations to come. Increasingly, we are coming to realise the illusion that we and our forebears have been living in.

We now have the knowledge and possibility to stand up and take our rightful place. We are, in a way, 'Light Bearers', Warriors of the Light. We live at an interesting time in history. Let your light shine.

The content of *Power of W: Women Thriving in Their Third Act* is structured as three phases which, I believe, represents a considered way, a path, for women to embark. I think that the initial words (as in the section on my story) are fitting to be written in Galicia, a Celtic region in Northern Spain, and with strong roots and connections to my native Ireland, a Celtic nation. In Galicia, on my most recent Camino to Finisterre, in September 2022, I received the inspiration to expand Part I – Conscious Presence, and include some words on topics that enter our thoughts but may seldom be given voice publicly.

I am an Irishwoman and have been living in Galway since 1993, on the west coast of Ireland by the Atlantic Ocean. My home is Limerick city, about 65 miles south of Galway. The ocean has always appealed to me and is where I draw my strength. So, walking on the shores of the Atlantic Ocean or bathing in its crystal waters, be it in Ireland, Portugal or Finisterre, Galicia, energises my spirit, connecting me to my source.

For me in writing this book the Irish, Celtic context is important. The Irish psyche of women is deeply rooted in our ancient past. A past where women were honoured as wise and wonderous, revered for their contribution to Irish life, community, and society. It is this power that we as Irish women need to reconnect with today, to embrace and reclaim, to bring us further into our true strength, as women of this day. This is not a power to dominate or subdue man. It is a power to connect with our own divinity – a power acknowledged and understood by those of our ancient past, roots bedded within our psyche. It would be glorious to bring these to the fore, alive once again, making whole ancient wisdom, creativity and divinity from our roots and weaving them into our current-day lives. We are a Celtic nation with roots in Druidic ways, descendants from the Tuatha Dé Danann (Divine Tribe of Light, people of Danu, the great earth goddess) with a mythic past – an ancient, powerful past where divine connection was understood, tuned and carefully aligned with nature and the seasons and sensing the sacredness of Mother Earth herself.

As an underlay to this book and the hope to honour my past, I wish to refer to an ancient woman from a powerful past. In these past generations women were whole in their lives and abilities, with deep sensitivity, creativity, femininity, intuition and mystical powers, understanding the divinity and wholeness of connection to all of life. A woman's marriage was not only to man and also her nurturing female role, but it was also a marriage of her spirit, her being, connecting her to the sacred and divine with all of life. Her truths were honoured and respected in society as a healer, psychic and teacher; her presence was sought after in her role as high priestess and wise woman, impacting on and contributing to the society of the times. It is with this brief description of this whole woman that I begin this book.

Some may be interested to know that the writing of this book started in my 63rd year. In chakra energy terms we are said to move in seven-year cycles – growing and evolving further with each cyclical iteration. For me this represents the ninth cycle. This may also be described as entering the final stage of life – a refining stage, the Third Act, and the stage that I might call the Wise Woman.

The themes presented on the following pages could be viewed as me being in my Third Act and this work representing a kind of culmination of my life to date. The first and second acts have already passed and what remains now is the Third Act. Hopefully, this phase of my life, which has already started, will be my best phase, with more awareness – building on the latter part of the second phase, where I had actively pursued my own personal growth and development. I now have a greater degree of space and the luxury to stop – to look back – to review and then step more consciously into each day of the Third Act.

This Third Act for me is very much connected with my contribution to life, part of a legacy so to speak. As I have no children, I have regarded this legacy to be my connection to people through my work and more so what I am bringing out from my work since I have reached 60+. The first of these creations is my book, *CARE of Leadership: A Practice for Developing Leadership Effectiveness*, and the training programme of the same name. The newest offerings are Reignite: The Retirement Ready Programme (training programme) and this book, *Power of W: Women Thriving in Their Third Act.* They have a deeper awareness focus, tapping into and opening to Spirit, our soul connection to Source (see above for a description of what is meant by this).

My hope is that the offerings presented through this latest book and my retirement-ready programmes and seminars will reach people on a path of conscious awakening and serve in some way to support the greater development of themselves and their gifts, as they let their unique light shine in the world. My wish is from this aspect of Being that they will fully experience and enjoy living in the light – shining their divinity through their unique divine expression.

2

How this Book Came to Be

Since the publication of my first book in 2017 I had been toying with the idea of authoring a book on women. I was not at all sure on the contents for the book; nevertheless the idea was sufficiently strong that I needed to give it further consideration. It would be a major departure for me as my first book, although it had personal development content, was still firmly classified as a business book. For the new book I knew that it would centre round the '3 Cs' – conscious presence, connection and contribution, and that was as far as it went.

During the inclement month of November 2018, while on the final section of Camino Francaise, Sarria to Santiago, having set the intention for my life's purpose to fully unfold and to ease my frustrations and anxiety that I may die without its unfoldment, let alone my fulfilment of it, the initial rumblings of the 3 Cs, my age of 63 and the onset of my Third Act finally collided. The initial sketchy ideas slowly started to float in, and I started to journal notes as they emerged for me over the next month. Extracts from these journal entries can be read in Section III.

In 2019, a structure to present the book dawned and the content started to develop. Was I finally ready to start in earnest with the book?

> 'If you want to make God laugh, tell him about your plans.'
>
> Woody Allen

Covid-19 intervened with a significant cascade of personal challenges following over the next years, culminating in July 2022. My life as I knew it was being stripped of every aspect that I held important. Only when these painful events were faced would I eventually be free in myself – free to be truly present to my Self.

The Camino in Finisterre in September brought me into greater alignment with my Self.

On 23 September 2022, I finally resumed my writing, reviewing what was written from years previously and then continuing with the writing to complete the manuscript on 21 October 2022.

3

Sections in the Book

Power of W: Women Thriving in Their Third Act introduces three concepts through what I refer to as the 3 Cs: Conscious Presence; Connection; and Contribution. I believe that the wholeness of women can be best seen with the engagement and fusion of these three Cs.

The phases of a woman's life (also depicted in the Triple Goddess) can be broadly categorised into maiden (early years); nurturer – encompassing the role of parent, carer, mentor, aunt, etc. (middle years); and 'crone' or, more acceptably, 'Wise Woman' (senior years). This latter phase is often characterised with wisdom, and I believe that this manifestation can typically emerge as the third C – contribution.

Power of W: Women Thriving in Their Third Act is presented in four sections. Part I, the current section, addresses the general introduction to the themes of the book, including how the book came to be, and the sections within the book.

Part II introduces the 3 Cs for the readers: Conscious Presence, Connection and, Contribution. The book then expands into a workbook format. Reflective questions contained within this section are intended to provide the reader with an opportunity to engage with the three concepts. The reader is encouraged to seek out actions for their unique journey that call to them from this exercise. This provides the opportunity for CARE (CA = Conscious Awareness, RE = Reflective Exercises)

– the approach previously adopted in my first book, *CARE of Leadership: A Practice for Developing Leadership Effectiveness.*

Part III presents my story and engagement with the three concepts. It also includes extracts from journal entries of the Caminos Francaise and Finisterre in 2018 and 2022. In St James' Cathedral, in Santiago, I set my Camino intention as that of direct conscious awakening. This, I felt, would truly propel me into the Third Act of my life – to one where I would feel fulfilled, living a life of joy and purpose: contributing. There was a lull in the writing work from 2019 to August 2022, during which a number of significant personal events arose.

Part IV presents some concluding comments. The 3 Cs weave together in the Third Act. Connecting with our True Self is key to finding out who we really are. Shining our gifts, our uniqueness into the world is essential; the importance of living authentically is emphasised. Finally, there is a reminder that change is an integral part of growth if we wish to live from our Authentic Self, in greater alignment with our True Self, allowing our true nature to emerge.

Within the Appendix that follows I have included a selection of tools and techniques which I hope will be helpful to you as you move through the material on your journey to wholeness.

4

Concluding Comments

Power of W: Women Thriving in their Third Act invites the reader to reflect on their lives, particularly as they transition into perhaps the most significant stage of their lives.

This Third Act presents great potential to fully engage with life. Choosing to live with passion, power and purpose opens up a life to be lived from the best version of oneself. It presents unlimited opportunity to fully embrace life. Expressing your individual uniqueness firstly through engagement with your gifts and talents, finding and living joyfully and then having the potential to express your light out into the world.

My story over the last couple of years, I hope, shows a life on a continuous conscious journey to grow and develop. My commitment to myself is to continually reach to the highest part of me for all the remaining days of my life.

I would love to hear from you on your amazing adventures.

PART II

The 3 Cs: Conscious Presence, Connection, and Contribution - Essentials for Us

5

Introduction

There is a gift hidden for us within our Third Act. Moving through the threshold, taking the initial steps towards this phase of our life, we have the opportunity to look back as well as forward. I am reminded of the phrase 'The past does not determine the future', and it seems particularly relevant at the start of this journey. It also serves as a reminder that we have choice; that we can, with awareness, make conscious choices. These choices will greatly influence our living in this Third Act when they are accompanied by congruent supporting actions which resonate with them.

This time, just now, as we embark on the Third Act, is the bridge between the past and the future. It serves as a time to pause, for review, re-evaluation, reclaiming and redefining who we are. It provides us with the space to assess what gives our life meaning and also to tap into our purpose. It allows us to question ourselves at the outset on how we are going to act in the newest phase of our lives and also what we are going to recreate.

We are standing at a unique time in our world's evolution. Our advances in the fields of science, medicine, wellbeing, technology and commerce have been spectacular. We have spanned the spectrum from a molecular level to outside our planet with our discoveries and inventions. Some have written that, in this time we are in now, our greatest discoveries will focus on an inward journey to ourselves.

This will involve connecting with our True Self, our True Essence, our divinity, part of the cosmic consciousness. These revelations will lead us to understanding and experiencing that we are immense beings, that we are a unique part of divinity, that we can express ourselves fully and completely in the amazing dance of living life to the full. Experiencing life from the emotions of love and joy, knowing that we are co-creators with the divine cosmic consciousness. Living life in this expanded state of awakened consciousness, living in wholeness as co-creators, is our birthright.

As I have mentioned in the Introduction, Part I, it is also an exciting time for women to move more fully into their power. For some this may well be a first and others may have already carved their way. This period of their lives may take on increasing significance.

In ancient Ireland, women played significant roles as nurturers, healers, and those gifted with psychic powers. Deep wisdom and a natural connection with the earth and Mother Nature herself were innate to these women. Their position in society was respected and honoured, with men often seeking their counsel.

For women now it might be a time to evaluate and see how their female skills and qualities can be harnessed more into engaging with communities on a global level, making more of a noteworthy influence to impact greater challenges facing people in all spheres of business and society. A time is fast approaching where nurturing, intuitive, creative and earthy grounding influences are needed to make the world a better place and to leave the world in a more sustainable state for future generations.

What follows is a suggested approach to getting started.

A good starting point would be to get a fix on where we are right now. As a preamble to finding ourselves it might be helpful to explore how we got here, to this point. We could consider performing a review, an assessment of the first two phases of our lives to date. What has our life been like up to now?

What might not go amiss in preparing for this undertaking is looking at our state of mind and the attitude with which we would embrace this study.

In such a study, adopting a neutral approach as much as possible would be wise. Embarking on this study from an observer's standpoint would be useful. It would be like you looking down on your life to date from afar, like someone who would be detached from the events and situations. Adopting this approach would be beneficial, particularly if there were events to be revisited which would have an emotional charge. Blame, resentment, anger and shame are some emotions which carry a negatively charged energy. These emotions may hinder and contaminate your view of events and situations as you look back on them now. This does not mean you are condoning or even dismissing them. Adopting the approach of an impartial observer is recommended. Where there are issues which have not been cleared up and/or you have not brought them to a satisfactory degree of closure, now would be an ideal time to address them, by yourself if you are qualified in this area, or else by seeking support. Failure to do so now perpetuates and prolongs your hurt.

Drawing a timeline of your life to date is one way to approach this review. In this exercise you can capture the highlights, achievements, strengths, and key points of your life. This timeline can also detail the challenges within this life. All of what preceded has influenced how we see ourselves and got us to where we are now.

There may well be many items from this review that you would wish to hold as precious and carry forward to your next phase. You may find that there could have been interests that you have left aside, things that you were passionate about, things that provided sources of joy and creativity, and that somehow, you have got disconnected from them. There may be strengths you may wish to hold, to further develop as you progress through the remaining years. Wholesome activities may be highlighted that you may wish to further expand. Having completed such an exercise, it would be good to check in and see how happy you are with yourself. If you are adventurous enough, you might consider looking into a mirror as you address this question.

It is important to make peace with yourself or indeed others. This is beneficial for you. It frees you up from the hurt that may otherwise imprison you. It is you who will be hurting otherwise. You owe this to yourself, now.

As you look at yourself from this vantage-point, how happy are you? How do you feel your best friend would describe you and introduce you to a perfect stranger?

Now, have you discovered any aspects from your past that are still niggling you? Is there something in a relationship or project that has been truncated, left unfinished?

Before getting into any of the questions that accompany this section, can you articulate what it is that you really want to get out of your life, starting this phase of your life?

Who are you now? This is not what others think you are. Nor is it the image that you might like to project into the world to meet the faces that you meet. Nor is it their expectations of you. These are others looking through their lenses and their perceptions. But they are not you.

This is really about who you believe you are and acknowledge yourself to be. Moving far beyond items accumulated to date, like your career, houses, cars, holidays, even hobbies, interests and accomplishments. It is about who you are at your core. You are a unique being on this planet expressing yourself as you are. You are one of a kind, no one else can do it as you do.

Looking inward, who are you really? Who are you in your quieter moments? What are your hopes and dreams? What do you want to express and experience in your lifetime? What fills you with joy?

In the exploration through the questions accompanying this section, you need to find out what it is you really want for your life, from this day forward. What is it that you want to feel, do and be?

6

First C: Conscious Presence

'To be beautiful means to be yourself. You don't need to be accepted by others. You need to accept yourself.'

Thich Nhat Hanh

Walk into a room with any number of people in it. Now think about what your entrance was like. Firstly, consider how others have felt and judged your presence. You may have taken note of the feedback received, both verbally and non-verbally. Now consider also how comfortable you are with being you, and who this you is just now. What energy vibrations are you emitting in relation to your confidence in your own skin? Your air can be easy, relaxed, and confident. Equally, it can be nervous and tinged with feelings of intimidation, unease and disharmony. Yet another option is that it could be angry and frustrated. The energy vibration that we emit can also be picked up by others.

The core of your vibration is important. It relates to the values which you hold, to your personality and to your leadership style. Your commanding presence is your personality, which you are expressing on an outer level. However, at a deeper level within you is your abiding presence. This part of you that remains unchanged, your conscious presence, connects you to your divine source. This source is the constant in your life. This is the Self, which embodies all love and never goes away – despite you hiding it. Through ego that Self can remain absent from your everyday life.

Your personality is a different aspect of you. It is the overcoat you wear to deal with the environment you are in and how you have, over the years, learned to cope with, interact with and influence this environment. Personality is a product – finely honed by you living your life. It is not permanent, it is not the real you and, like an overcoat, it can get worn and torn – and then needs to be shed. Sometimes, though, we become attached to this coat. And wear it well after the sell-by date – well after its usefulness has ended. Stuck in the pattern of the familiar, the overcoat becomes shabby and does not do justice to the real you – this permanent you is different, it is all-loving and has been hidden by your personality.

You may need to stop and assess whether your life, your reality, is cloudy and dirty and in need of a clean-up. The lens of your perception affects your thoughts and how you interact with and see yourself in the invention you have chosen to live within.

This lens of perception is only a view – but not the real view, not the real you.

Others too are looking at the world through their specific lens. These combined lenses can make up a complex tapestry of the world, which is not real in the first place. However, people fight vehemently to not only hold their view of the world but also to impose this view on others – judging situations and events through their lens, the values and standards held by them as correct – which may be their truth, but not necessarily the Truth.

Many wars have been created in relationships, families and communities by such rigid views held by self-righteous beliefs.

Looking beneath the surface, connecting with the Real, takes time. Finding peace and abiding presence is the gift presented through this connection.

Connecting regularly enables you to shine your light more into the world – it brings you into true states of confidence, reflecting more your true essence, not the ego-confidence, which is shallow and driven by selfishness.

However, shining this light may be a source of concern to others. Uncomfortable with it, they may take this as an attack and even react by attacking themselves.

Commitment to this deeper exploration and connection to it can often be a lonely path. It is a path less travelled by others, and as it has not been explored by them it can become a source of separation because it can lead to a plethora of abuses from others: hurling negativity, disowning their Truth and instead projecting their fears in all their guises, including the fear of you coming into the light – for leaving their world and perhaps seeing you as different, not like them. The result is the end of the relationship, shutting you down, cutting you off as alien and not living by the right view, their view, of the world.

Maintaining your presence and connectedness to the deeper personal aspect of you is important – once found, it is a prize worth having and holding dear.

This deeper journey and connection offer the gifts of confidence and peace, which in turn emanate from you. This is also the place where compassion and forgiveness abide.

For your understanding of their misunderstanding, coupled with their judgement, is not placing you higher than others. Rather it is a place where you hold this knowledge of the greater Truth – the truth where peace and love abide.

The place that is less travelled, but once opened to you, is the abiding presence. The light from this place may dazzle, blinding others – but often it may be the source of curiosity, giving others the opportunity to see their unique connection and expression in the world.

The initial stepping out into this presence can be a bit daunting – but soon increases in absorbing the pieces of negation, the fear of shining forth, of shining afresh your uniqueness. You relax into your connectedness and the expression of divinity within you.

Conscious Presence is sought through awareness and being in the present moment. It is not a future state, it is time in no time, there is only the present moment – there is no other gift. In this present time, we need to live to the highest standard of which we are capable. So, our mission, our purpose is to choose the best possible version of ourselves for a given conscious moment. If this moment has been deemed by us to be a less than perfect state, then we can consciously choose to change and reach for the next highest state in the next moment, which then becomes the present moment. So, as we live in each present moment and each of these flow into another, we can choose to live in fullness within the highest possible state: in the abiding presence of the present moment. Self-awareness is the key to such living.

Living in this state we become more of our Authentic Self. We drop the stories that bind us to ego and illusion. We become more realistic and aligned with our True Self – the unchanging and unbounded self, the state where love, joy and compassion abide. We come to know our True Self.

In the quieter moments of this inner connection, the new and more authentic you can emerge. Even though these may be your very first steps, there is a knowledge within you that it needs to shine forth. This knowing, shaky and weak, is yet a purposeful awakening. The ego, in its fear-based place, can slowly have its veil parted reluctantly. With persistence there will be a yielding to this greater power. Ever-increasing degrees of the Authentic You surface as you step up to claim centre stage, with the final act to be played – living and shining your incandescent light. Your uniqueness expresses itself from the vulnerable yet purposeful delicate first steps to claiming a power, a rightful place for your splendid magnificence to shine ever forth.

These steps will help you to finally feel your strength with almost paradoxical fear and yet confident knowing that you, through surrendering, have arrived in this centred part of you which is your splendid magnificence – divinity shining forth in your unique and gifted presence to the world.

In taking these first steps, with a fragment of the ego remaining, there may be old doubts, almost clinging disbelief about this expansion experienced within you. Somehow, from the depth, a careful, confident, caring conscious voice gives the gentle nudge encouraging more steps – supporting through its reassuring presence until the more confident, centred you is finally established, freeing you to sing your song and shine your splendour more assuredly from this anchored, trusted place. With the final clutches of shattered ego falling away, yielding to the magnificence of the light casting rays to all who enter its presence of abiding grace, the True and Authentic You is living from the conscious present moment.

From this place the past collapses, doubts dissolve, a graceful loving presence takes hold, anchoring you in this light for you to engage in experiences through your unique expression. The emerging, more confident, quieter you connects consciously with your gifts and now shares in your world.

From here you walk in this abiding presence, secure, centred, your steps are joyous in this blissful knowledge. Moving out, moving forth with unshakeable belief in your sacred space – your sacred Self.

The wonder of our life and the coming home to our true identity is an ongoing personal evolution, evolving in spiritual awareness into the reality of Who We Really Are. We cannot always choose what happens in life, but we have a choice about how we respond to whatever happens. George Orwell sums this up with the following quote:

'Happiness can only exist in Acceptance.'

Connecting with who you really are and the retirement phase of your life presents an interesting discussion. I believe, regardless of how adjusted one is, that approaching this phase becomes a bit scary. Yes, there were many retirements over the course of one's life – retiring at any age as you leave one phase of life and enter the next: teenage year to adulthood, moving into third-level education, moving away from home, entering the workforce, changing jobs, getting promoted, moving home, getting married, getting divorced, becoming a parent, becoming a grandparent. The list has many different 'retiring' aspects to it. However, entering the Third Act does call for a reality check. You are getting a call to attention. A call to check in on how you are up to now and a call to let you know you can have space for an even greater life. The key to this is held in understanding Who You Really Are and that you can be all you desire if you believe in yourself – everything is possible. You are an aspect of the divine and your reason for existing is to express yourself in your unique way.

This connection with Who You Really Are looks for the True Self rather than the Ego Self. It can be experienced as true moments of awareness with the alignment of Who We Really Are – True Self that emanates from our core, uniting with the pure essence of love.

The awareness of others through one's lens of the Third Act can sometimes bring divergence as you find your intentions of connecting with others far adrift from your actual actions. This can be somewhat upsetting, as you wanted to operate from a higher level of consciousness. Despite the fact that you wish to get more in touch with your goodness and essence, this does not translate to what plays out in reality. Who is acting from this space? Is it really you? Sometimes you may not even know it is you who is acting out. Yes, it is you, the egoistic self from a dark, distant past that has a voice, that has remained hidden, unheard, and wanting expression. This voice needs to be embraced, listened to and acknowledged. It is a part of you coming to be healed. This healing might require actions from others and yet you have no control over their actions.

Somehow you need to bring this to the fore in your life, supporting yourself with whatever healing is needed. It is also important to surrender and be accepting of what is now and to finally bring the issue/s to rest. With this care of yourself you can heal – a healing which is well overdue, one that is nurturing and cocooning you, a healing coming from the core of you to love yourself through the acceptance of what has happened and move you into more wholeness now. Moving you closer to the unfoldment of your Authentic Self – more in alignment with your true essence.

Briefly let us turn to the word 'power', which appears in the title of this book and is referenced throughout. You may well ask: 'How can I describe myself as powerful?'

What I am referring to is the power that you have over yourself and your actions – personal power (self-empowerment). This is a very different power to the external power which relatively few people have been given. However, self-empowerment is available to all of us.

It is evident when we take control of our lives using power to overcome life's obstacles, follow our dreams and desires, and seek fulfilment. Self-empowerment is intrinsically linked to our true essence with a source where infinite possibilities are available to us.

> 'Most of the shadows of this life are caused by standing in one's own sunshine.'
>
> Ralph Waldo Emerson

The Divine Feminine is a subject which is receiving increasing interest and one which I would like to briefly touch on. As I too was interested in this subject, I attended a workshop on the Divine Feminine in the Algarve late 2021. I deepened my interest and practice by drawing on resources from the Chopra Center on Divine Feminine mediations. The Divine Feminine, we are told, is rising and this is good. However, in some male circles this subject has caused some unrest and confusion.

Within each of us, no matter how we present ourselves, the subtle energies of masculine and feminine exist. The masculine energies can be described as solar, warming and active, while the feminine energies on the other hand are lunar, cooling and receptive. Masculine energies have been the dominant force of how to get on and be successful in the world for centuries, next to the suppression of the feminine energies. Now at this time there is a rebalancing of energies with the rise of the feminine energy, the Divine Feminine and the restoration of balance both within us and also in the external world. This is not a revolt. On the contrary, the energy of the Divine Feminine brings to the fore the qualities of joy, love, compassion, empathy, nurturing, creativity, intuition, and peace.

Unspoken topics

Before closing this section on conscious presence, there might be merit in raising a number of topics generally left unspoken. For some women, these topics can often enter their thoughts and become sources of stress. Without acknowledgement this can be distressing, borne out by the lack of airing and discussion of these topics. The resulting problem is that women can feel alone and isolated by thinking that there is something amiss with them because these topics are not raised in a public setting.

So, let us look at a sample of these.

Lack of sex after 50+

Entering menopause can be considered a stage of sexual freedom. The possibility of pregnancy has been eliminated and the enjoyment of sex can be enhanced. This is a liberating experience for most women, feeling truly comfortable with their expression in sexual union without holding back. A woman at this stage is still alive and vital, with many more years yet to enjoy life.

However, a lack of sex and/or spontaneity, the habit of schedule now becoming the ritual, is also a common experience for women at this stage of life. You might question this mechanical, boring act that you are going along with: what for? Your desires are being swamped. All the while you are losing more and more of your essential self. The pain of containing your desire to be heard now far outweighs the fear of staying in a stalemate. Exposed now, it is inevitable to act even if it means being on your own and moving on from a situation that you know you have outgrown. Yes, the uncertainty now is more appealing than the stale and certain death, life without passion in an intimate relationship as the ultimate certainty. Does any of the above sound familiar to you?

In other cases, the restored freedom and enthusiasm of menopause may not be welcomed by a partner. For example: the partner may not desire to engage in sex from this point onwards. For others, when they do engage, it may be infrequent and/or lack spontaneity and variety. All these scenarios can leave women feeling abandoned, unattractive, deprived, cast aside, unworthy and a host of other feelings as a result of this reduced interest and infrequency of intimacy. The net result leads to frustration. This may also be combined with the fear of addressing this subject with the partner out of a fear of the outcome. This build-up causes stress not only for the woman, but the partnership suffers also.

This situation is made more complex as women may feel that they are completely isolated, because this is not generally a topic discussed by women.

Finding your voice

Have you ever heard the sound of your own voice? If yes, how comfortable are you with hearing it?

Oftentimes we are fearful of raising and voicing our opinions. We also are often fearful of declaring our needs and the accompanying emotions around these unexpressed needs. This fear can relate to how others would be affected and in turn to their reactions. Often fear can arise with what was said and now being unable to retract it, unable to erase it without a trace of fearing the avalanche effects on another's life. But now how you live is going to be affected as you own the truth of what was voiced. This fear can often be coupled with a greater fear: that of change. It is you now out there, carrying and forging ahead with your life. You are living life now, on your own terms: you are free to explore your world and leave your footprint saying that you have lived.

For women particularly when entering the last phase of life – whether one had a career to this point, was a homemaker or had other roles, or some combination of roles – this time of life is regarded as freeing. Finding your voice is an essential contribution to living a fulfilled life, whether you are in a relationship with a significant other or single. Negotiating this segment of life requires you to be seen and heard, you are a unique being. You matter; your presence is significant to the world. Therefore, if you have not taken steps for your voice to be heard apart from the crowd, community, or family, this is your time. This time is calling you, with no room in your life now to play small.

If up to now you have been playing yourself down, perhaps because you were with a dominant partner who regularly voiced their opinions and views, you may have adopted them as 'truth' without even questioning them. Choosing not to have an independent opinion, you were accepting to see the world through the lens of someone else. Holding them in a raised state as the sole source of knowledge, you were giving your power away.

For some it may be daunting even to hear your own voice as you speak out your ideas, opinions, dreams and desires. So, shake off the background person, and give voice to what you value. This may cause a few raised eyebrows. Some may be surprised, either positively or negatively, with this newfound you.

In turn, this can take some adjustment for both you and the others. The key is to continue to wear this new oversized coat and get used to filling it. Continue on, and as you do you will grow more confident with this latest version of you. You may also take the opportunity to further support yourself – by learning more about yourself and the way you interact with others. Many courses can be found in this regard. You may decide to start a short course in your local area on assertiveness, confidence and influencing people.

Changing could be likened to throwing a pebble in a pond – it produces ripples as it radiates outwards. Others are affected by the change. It will require some action or interaction on their part. Some will be surprised and positively disposed to the newest version of you. Others, however, may not – but you need to stick to your guns. Negotiate the relationship between the two of you. In the end the relationship will move to a new place, or it could be truncated. Just remember you only have control over yourself. You cannot change another person. So, whatever their response or reaction to you is, they are entirely in charge of their side of the relationship. It is their business, so to speak. You have to look after your business only, your side of the relationship. Hopefully, all will move nicely along. However, if this is not the case, you may need to review and renegotiate the relationship. Sometimes it could even wind up with the relationship breaking up. Sad as this may be, you need to honour yourself in the relationship and respect the other person.

Relationships are not always meant to last a lifetime once they start. Sometimes we attract people into our lives for a reason and maybe for only a defined period of time, then both move our separate ways. The thing is not to cling to a relationship that is not serving one's best interest or both parties' interests. Holding on to such relationships may embitter either one or both parties. Blessing the relationship for what it has given you would be a good thing to do, and then gently let it go. Hurting in a relationship only leads to embitterment. It is always best to give from a loving heart – otherwise your friendship is not love-based but some kind of trading or conditional love.

Feelings of being 'past it'

- *'The good years are gone now and I'm definitely looking the worse for wear.'*
- *'What is the use of picking myself up now?'*
- *'I am bulging out in too many places.'*
- *'My face is bearing the tales of the years. There are so many wrinkles ... It is no use anyway.'*
- *'Sure, for what! No one has taken any notice of me lately.'*

Do any of these have a familiar ring to them?

Yes, the years have progressed. If this type of thinking is affecting your mood and behaviour, you owe it to yourself to do something about it. There is no point in compounding the misery. This is unnecessary suffering. It can be avoided. No one will thank you for it. Quite the opposite: often this will alienate people from you.

So, take a first step by promising yourself to stop filling your head with this negativity. Eliminate these thoughts, replacing them with more life-affirming thoughts: ones that are gentle on yourself, and definitely more uplifting. Start forming a new set of neural pathways – ones that support you, that are life-affirming.

As you move into caring more for yourself, you might start by setting realistic goals in relation to your appearance and, more importantly, your mindset. It is all about you taking care of you.

Your presence with your significant other – problems

As we move into the Third Act the nature of our intimate relationships can change. For some people, retirement can strengthen their relationship with their significant other, as they spend more time together and renew their connection to one another without the distractions of children and work. For others, little changes and the relationship continues along the same track as before. And for a third group of people, this may be a time in which cracks in their intimate relationship, which were previously glossed over, come to the fore. In this scenario feelings may not be adequately voiced, and instead people learn to forget in an effort to move on in the relationship. But is it really moving on? The reality can be that we get stuck in a groove; trust gets eroded even with the best intention of forgiving the other.

Often a deep dive is required in intimate relationships to re-establish our values, what is important to us as individuals, to see who we really are and also to see the other.

This deep dive can be put off, possibly because of fear and what life would be like without the other person. Moving 'forward' is often justified by statements like 'we have differences, but we always seem to make up and move forward.'

But what if the moving forward and staying together actually stunts our own growth? The result of the decision to stay together is that a little bit of you gets lost in these rows and upsets. Slowly and systematically, you are numbing yourself – your True Self. Slowly but steadily, you move to deaden the small voice within calling you home to your True Self. But even this faint version of your voice is never so soft that it cannot be heard. It never gives up on you and in quieter moments of your life it continues to call. This beckoning is stronger than the pull of the relationship. What is needed from you is to remove the blinkers. Assess the relationship, particularly your part in it. What is important and valuable to you? Have you tried your best? Was your intention pure? After the analysis, the next step is seeking a discussion with the other person. Often external intervention is needed if there is a keen sense that the relationship can be salvaged. This case is one where you still can remain true to yourself. Other times, even with these efforts, the relationship sadly must end.

Feelings of failure with relationship breakdown

When a relationship, a marriage or a long-term partnership breaks down, this often brings with it the gnawing sense of failure. We need, however, to adopt a more realistic viewpoint. Relationships in our great-grandparents' time were often of a shorter duration in comparison to the potential span of today's world. The reality is we are living much longer, and the result is that the lifetime of a marriage/relationship has extended significantly. It is common to see a marriage/relationship span 60+ years. But it is also increasingly common now to see breakups and multiple relationships develop for an individual over a similar time span.

People grow and evolve throughout their lifetime and therefore it is possible that one could outgrow a marriage or partnership. Taking this a step further, it is reasonable to argue that as a person negotiates the various phases of life, and their situation evolves, 'the one' might not be 'the one' at all these various stages. So, it is wonderful if a couple can start out together and wind up together for a lifetime, thinking of each other still as 'the one' and still being in love. This is possible when two people consciously work on the relationship, negotiate each phase, and still grow together in the relationship.

Another scenario is where a couple stays together, but, in reality, they have a 'married singles' arrangement if you look beneath the surface. The relationship has stagnated along the way. They merely have fallen into the habit of being together but without any quality to the relationship. Possibly the feeling is that of 'it is not worth the hassle of separating.' They have drifted apart emotionally.

So, instead of feeling that a significant relationship has failed, having put in a conscious effort to work on it, it might be better to view this differently. It could be that one party has in fact outgrown this relationship. The time has come to move forward alone. Other relationships that resonate more with their growth stage may then appear in their path. They now have the potential to form another relationship with a more compatible partner, one with whom growing the relationship is possible, both parties evolving individually and likewise the relationship continuing to grow.

Internalised misogyny

Women's career progression was often halted by the forces of the invisible ceiling. Often being passed over by other colleagues just because of their gender. Women, regardless of their competence, were seen as lesser and were often dealt with unfairly in relation to promotion just because of their sex. Another factor, though not voiced, was that women of 'childbearing years' were often passed over. Through the introduction of employment legislation in more recent times these injustices have been stemmed. However, other situations have come to the surface. Take the scenario of a woman in a position of power dealing out injustices unpleasantly to others of the same sex. She could and can stunt the promotional path of other women because of jealousy and biases; sometimes the phrase 'pulling up the ladder behind you' can apply in these situations. These situations unfortunately often remain unvoiced because of the ensuing repercussions. Also, and quite bizarrely, the general reaction would be almost incredulous disbelief that one woman would be subjected to this treatment by another woman.

Due to petty jealousy and feelings of inferiority toward her (because of her looks, figure, dress, the way she carries herself, her confidence and attitude in social and business settings), a woman may 'have a go' at another woman, castigating her and putting her down, either verbally, with other women, or even just through her thoughts. Both are energy attacks on the recipient.

Where is the generosity of spirit in doing this?

Perhaps you may have acted in this way at some stage. With awareness now you may reflect on the questions at the end of this chapter to discover the trigger for you. Then take appropriate steps to heal the wound and cultivate a more generous spirit.

Evolving and Growth

This theme naturally flows from the growth of individuals, which means both parties in the relationship are interested in developing, growing and evolving, firstly as individuals and then as a couple in a relationship. The reality is that all relationships need work if they are to survive and thrive. With only one party doing the work while the other abstains, for whatever reason, even with the best will in the world it is unlikely that the relationship will be sustained.

There are three apparent choices available to the individual wishing to develop. The first is to accept the situation totally, allowing the other person to be as they are and continue only with their own growth without questioning the other. This is a lot easier said than done. It means being totally accepting and not reacting to the other person's actions or behaviour. The second option is to try to change the situation through communication between the parties and/or external intervention and follow through with actions and solutions to re-establish the relationship. This involves time, effort and a willingness from both parties to get the relationship more than just back on track. This action results in a better, improved relationship with a commitment to continually work on the relationship. The third and final option is to let the relationship go completely. This is a dramatic event for anyone.

The stages for dealing with such an emotional event are encompassed in the acronym SARAH, which is discussed in the Appendix.

Let us work through these stages with Joanna in the following scenario.

- **S**HOCK – Joanna is totally in shock as she receives the unbearable news that her partner, George, wants out of the relationship. This has come like a bolt, unexpectedly.
- **A**NGER – Joanna is angry with George for a host of reasons, including his failing to discuss his feelings and issues. It might also be that Joanna turns her anger inwards on herself – for not reading the signals and not spotting this sooner.

Joanna is hurt with the coldness of George's delivery of seeking an end to the relationship. She thinks about all the times she felt wronged by him, about the violation, betrayal and erosion of trust.

Joanna is hurt at the foolishness of staying in the relationship and thinks about the many times she had not voiced adequately or had stifled what needed to be said. She had thought maybe not saying too much would be easier, for George's sake. In doing this Joanna was not honouring herself.

- **R**EJECTION – Joanna rejects the breakdown of the relationship. She starts rationalising the situation. She reconciles the information and explains it away. She experiences the defensive response 'it is not my fault' and lays the blame on George.
- **A**CCEPTANCE – Joanna now reaches acceptance – not from the Ego Self but from a deeper place. She experiences a surrendering to what is. Her thinking might include that the Divine has a greater plan.

  In the past she may have thwarted this by slavishly following the insatiable Ego, which only knows fear. Fear either of losing what one has or of not getting what one wants. Either way the Ego just generates fear.

  Only when Joanna comes to that place of acceptance and surrender does she truly find peace. Peace may not come all at once, but through grace and surrender, one step at a time, does one finally break free from the grip of the Ego.
- **H**EALING – Finally Joanna reaches the last stage, which is healing. In this stage the past no longer holds the hurt. For Joanna, awareness of the present moment is now possible. Surrender and acceptance now take over. Joanna finds that peace is present, living is easier. Resistance has faded, giving way to accepting what is in front of her.

  She follows the subtle hints and stepping-stones laid in front of her. She finds that with awareness, by being present, it is easier not only to see them but also to act on them, with each one leading her gently forward. Joanna is led to peace and serenity – to a new dimension which is ever-present and unfolding in the Now.

Death

Preamble

The transition into the last phase of life, our Third Act, brings our mortality into sharp focus. Given the busyness of life today and the way life is lived by most at a hectic pace, there seems to be little time for reflection, let alone to talk about death.

As we look around our environment, nature clearly points out the natural cycle of life, moving through the seasons. We, on the other hand, address death by brushing it off, something to be shunned and certainly not spoken about. It is as if we run from death, failing to see that if we don't give it consideration we miss the opportunity of its potential to bring focus to our life: becoming more mindful and conscious of the gift of each day.

Death is one of the greatest unspoken subjects. Do you disagree with me on this one? Well, for most people, when they think about death it usually is in relation to someone else who is dying or has just passed.

So, the question to put to ourselves is: do we really think about death in relation to ourselves? Death can at any moment take our breath away, at any hour of any day. It is the ever-present shadow which is with all of us. I'm reminded of John O'Donohue's *Anam Cara* and the section 'Death as an invitation', where he says:

> 'When you think about it you should not let yourself be pressured by life. You should never give your power to a system or to other people. You should hold the poise, balance, and power of your soul within yourself.'

A wise person will totally embrace that death is inevitable. Death actually gives us a wake-up call. In so doing, it presents us with the challenges to live life fully and live to our highest potential.

What would you do if you were told that you had only one month left to live? How would you feel about this? Would it change your priorities? What things would you like to do? Who would you meet? How would you interact with them?

Maybe develop the wise person within you. Treat each day as if it was going to be your last. By adopting this approach and mindset, your awareness enables you to live life to your highest potential every moment of each day. Having embraced life in this way, in response to the question 'What would you do if you were told you had only one month left to live?' you could say that there was not a single thing that you would rather be doing with your life. Simply put, you are living your life fully: not making any compromises in living to your potential and totally at peace with yourself.

Every moment matters.

So, if you are not living this way, ask yourself why. You know that death is inevitable. We just don't know when.

Start today and make changes to how you live your life. Commit to living every moment and let nothing stop you.

> 'We are intellectually concerned with the idea of awareness, yet not actually aware of what is taking place.'
>
> Krishnamurti

Conscious Presence Questions

With the questions that follow, you have an opportunity for reflection on where you are in your life now. You may also consider what actions, if any, you may like to take following your review and response to these questions.

Keeping a regular journal may be beneficial.

When deciding on the actions needed, you may wish to put these into the SMART goal format as referenced in the Appendix. It is worthwhile to be specific about the results you wish to achieve and also to set out the tasks needed and arrange them in a logical timeframe.

As a starting point for your reflections on Conscious Presence, review and document your responses to this set of questions.

Question 1

- How would you describe or introduce yourself?
- How do you come across in a business setting?
- How do you come across with family and friends?
- How do you think your partner/significant other would describe you?
- How would you describe yourself in your quieter moments, when you are alone with yourself?
- Do you feel connected with something greater than you? Can you describe this? What does this do for you?

Identify five values that you hold. State why they are important to you.

Question 2

- As you look back on your life today, from this vantage point, how comfortable are you with your life to date? Are there any areas with which you are not comfortable with? Describe these in detail.
- Are there any changes you would like to make that are within your control? Identify three actions which you would like to take to make improvements and to which you can commit.

Question 3

- What dreams have you discounted because of more pressing and immediate situations or because the time was not right? Are these dreams still beckoning to you?
- You may feel that it is too late or that you may look foolish embarking on these now. You are never too old to follow your dreams. Start now, do not waste another minute. Do not let the opportunity go by and have deep regrets later.

Question 4

- You may have been bestowed with creative talents which you have truncated because of money or time pressures, such as writing, painting, crafts, dance, etc. Is it now time for you to reconnect with these?

Question 5

- Have faraway travel and exploration appealed to you, but such expense did not seem sensible?

Question 6

- Is there a relationship that is fractured and may require you to take the first brave step in attempting to mend it?

Question 7

- Are there any charitable projects that may benefit from your involvement but that you may have been slow to volunteer for to date?

Question 8

- How do you view death? Describe your thoughts and fears. Is there anything you would do now if you knew you had only six months left to live?

Question 9 – Challenge

- For the next 21 days, keep a Gratitude Journal. Fill in at least three things for which you are grateful each day. On the completion of each daily entry, notice how you feel.
- In the section below, describe the overall benefits to you for completing this 21-day process.

Question 10 – Unspoken Section

- Having reviewed the examples in this section, did any one of these resonate with you? Journal about it firstly and then enter actions which you wish to take over the next three, six and twelve months.

7

Second C: Connection

'Marriages, even the best ones – perhaps especially the best ones – are an ongoing process of spoken and unspoken forgiveness.'

Dalai Lama XIV

'You show your humanity by how you see yourself not as apart from others but from your connection to others.'

Desmond Tutu

From *The Book of Joy: Lasting Happiness in a Changing World*

When connecting with others, the key ingredient for successful relationships is to be present. Awareness, or being present to each moment, is the principle to follow when connecting with others. It supports the growth and deepening of all your relationships and in return is an essential ingredient for your own development and growth and for connecting to your True Self.

At the heart of successful connections is effective communication. In these interactions, 'Deep Listening' is central to success. It involves being truly present: the focus is solely on what is going on in the interaction, moment by moment. Awareness is essential. Deep listening is listening not just to the words and their meaning but to the emotions behind them as well. It is also about noticing the unspoken words and feelings. It is about giving full attention to the person and listening with your heart (Chopra).

In effective interactions, judgement is suspended. Understand that each person is operating at their own level of consciousness. We are not separate. We are all one Divine Light.

Creating healthy boundaries is important in all our connections and relationships. In relationships, giving can only be true if it comes from a loving heart. We therefore must make sure that the well of love within ourselves is full before giving to others. We need to be constantly replenishing this well within us and nourishing ourselves. Giving to others from this well that is not full is not true giving.

Our various relationships will be discussed in the following sections.

In closing, trying to attract a relationship or a situation based only on the ego may bring some limited results, but it will not be fulfilling, long-lasting, or in your best spiritual interests, because the ego mind comes from a state of lack and limited understanding.

Connections – with Parents

In the later years of our parents' lives, they may feel that they have become a burden. If you are in your Third Act and your parents are still part of your life, have you ever wondered what this is about?

Sometimes there can be a role reversal, with the child adopting a parental role and vice versa, in these relationships. Is there a grand design to our parents living into old age like this? Are they still with us to do some healing in the relationship between us?

Growing old and the ageing process for parents when we are in our Third Act can be exceedingly difficult for both parties, but especially for them. So, perhaps it may be beneficial for us to see their staying with us as a gift – an unspoken gift, maybe an unconscious contract between us. It is up to us, the children, to see if there is any healing that needs to be done around the relationship. To clear up any remaining loose ends. The relationship resolution allows for forgiveness, the release of any painful, relived and recycled memories. Then it is possible to enter a renewed, refreshed and more conscious loving relationship – both as adults. Maybe, indeed, this is for the first time. A loving, giving, serving, respectful relationship, one that honours both, one that connects us and aligns us with our true essential nature, is one to be cherished.

For either party in this relationship, it may be the first time in a long while to hear the comforting, heartfelt words 'I love you'. It is wonderful to hear them as coming from a loving place, a loving nature, and equally important is acceptance and letting these words into your being. To finally feel and experience the wondrous flow of pure love is miraculous.

With parents still living, we may now be caring for a parent or certainly providing some form of support. This may be our chance to give back something to a mother who suffered labour pains to give us the gift of life. It may be another opportunity to express gratitude to both our mother and father for the care and love we received in our dependent years.

All families, regardless of how loving the environment was, can have issues. This, as seen by us, can be how we have perceived and experienced the situation. Still, carrying our hurt and perception of wrongdoing into the present is not healthy for anyone. These incidences occurred well in the past, a lot of water has flown under the bridge in the intervening time. We are, after all, adults now in our Third Act. So, if we are carrying hurt, this needs to be addressed. Forgiveness is important. We are finally freeing and releasing ourselves, ending the hurt that was damaging us. This release and forgiveness will also be gratefully felt by the parent concerned.

Connection with Siblings

Hearing one's own siblings narrate their stories and memories of their experiences within one's family of origin can be an interesting exercise. Sometimes, one would be forgiven for thinking, was this the same family that I was part of? Stories, when unfolded, reveal the intricacies of the individual, highlighting the point and the importance placed on each one being a unique individual. Our experience of the same event can be, and has been, viewed through a uniquely different lens. The reactions to these events are also unique because of the interactions, experiences and patterns that have preceded such an event. Revisiting an event experienced by siblings can reveal vastly different interpretations. This then colours their judgement and influences their dealings and interactions with parents, other siblings, and relationships external to the family of origin.

Where you are positioned in the family also has a bearing on your siblings, in the form of sibling interactions. For example, being the eldest in a large family, one may have had to take on responsibility, performing household family duties at a relatively early age. This role was adopted more than likely to share the normal family duties as a way of easing the workload of the parents. It is reasonable to think that, in such a scenario, this eldest child would have grown up more quickly. This child would have become more independent, adopting leadership roles and also having greater care and consideration for others. Taking on such responsibilities may also have influenced the child's personality, with them tending to be more serious in outlook. This child may be seen as being more diligent at school. In relation to money, this child may have started being more careful and frugal about spending. Being influenced by and adopting parental norms well before their time, they perhaps were missing the fun and playful aspects of life that other children of their age were able to enjoy.

A unique aspect of the eldest child would have been testing boundaries as they were seeking out new experiences growing up in their world. They may have been blazing trails, pushing boundaries and forging and forming new norm rules which would benefit the younger family members as they reach their own milestones of growing up within the family.

All of these activities and events colour personality, they build and develop your experiences. They write the unique story of your growing years within the family.

As a middle child, you would no doubt have a separate set of experiences. It may have been a position in which you felt you received less attention than others. You may have felt that you were forgotten about.

If this was your reality you may have sought out ways or activities that enabled you to get the attention you needed, or you may have disappeared a bit.

As a younger child, you may have been bestowed with great love and affection throughout all of your growing years. Things would have come easier to you. People may have smothered you, so to speak – in the process of caring too much. This may have resulted in your fending less for yourself. In later years this may have left you less equipped for dealing with challenges in the world and an independent life.

So today, as you look from your own lens at your current phase of life, it is an opportunity to see if there are patterns in your habitual ways of interacting and connecting with your siblings. This may then prompt you to make some adjustments in an effort to make relationships more whole.

Seeking out any type of needs, such as acknowledgement, say, from parents still living, may indeed still be on an individual's agenda. Judgement and competition may still be actively alive within a sibling's mind. Continued rivalry may be misplaced in the present life experience, however, awareness may not have dawned. Messages from the past events may not have moved on. Without being addressed there is no resolution, let alone learning, acknowledgment and acceptance. Still operating from the past mode, wheels spinning and not going anywhere, this child (now adult) remains stuck. The result is that they only contaminate the present and lose the opportunity of building a more loving relationship. With the ego still reigning, a dark shadow is cast on the Light and blocking it from shining forth.

Connection with Your Significant Other

Focusing on your relationship with your significant other is important now. It may very well need plentiful servings of TLC. It may result in questions surfacing, raise fears and be a source of concern as you explore this relationship further. For women in their Third Act, it may very well pose questions of a physical nature as well as mental, emotional and spiritual. It is hoped that, through exploration and the resulting findings, it will be the initiation leading to reach a greater understanding of you in this relationship. Further work with the findings may flow from this.

It may also be worthwhile to revisit Part II – First C: Conscious Presence, and also within that the section 'Lack of Sex After 50+'.

Within the relationship circle, your relationship with your significant other needs to be given crucial importance. After all, it is your primary relationship after the relationship you have with yourself. The relationship with your significant other is the relationship you have chosen and the one that will afford the most growth potential for you. In this relationship, like no other, you are constantly provided with a mirror that is being held up to you. These romantic, intimate relationships are the vehicle by which emotions are magnified' (Tony Robbins), both the negative as well as the positive, and as such provide the greatest opportunity to grow and evolve.

If you and your partner got together at an early age, you may have had children and, generally speaking, their rearing would have involved a sizeable portion of your available time – leaving little time for your relationship together. The demand on your time in bringing up a family can never be underestimated. Caring for their physical, mental, emotional and spiritual wellbeing may have stretched you to your limit over a twenty-year period or so. Now however, the kids have grown up, out on their own now and are carving out their individual lives. Now you are on your own again as a couple.

Finding yourself in the Third Act with your partner may present something of an interesting journey, to say the least. Your role as a mother is less in the foreground. Of course, you will always be a mother, but this role and its responsibility has been significantly lessened.

Now it is just the two of you, alone together as a couple again after many years. You are now in an unfamiliar environment again, and both of you are in your Third Act.

While this time in your life may be freeing, it may also raise some questions and these could lead to some anxiety perhaps, or at least a period of questioning. The fact that you are still together now comes into sharper focus.

Some searching questions may arise at this time, with the most obvious being whether or not you still want to continue to be together now. Were the intervening years with your focus on the family a mask for you to hide your true relationship with your partner? Now is perhaps a time for you to explore how you feel in this newest phase of your relationship and whether or not it is still okay for you to be here in it. Have you outgrown each other, or have you moved together, lived and grown both individually and as a couple? This may well be a time to have some introspection. Have a deep conversation with your partner to establish your willingness and commitment to continue your union. Staying together and living in a half-life, not daring to address your relationship and make a conscious decision about it, could be a cause for regret. Down the road there could be remorse for missing the opportunity to make this conscious choice. Drifting is also a choice – albeit less conscious.

Another aspect of viewing your relationship is related to you questioning perhaps your image and how you think your partner sees you now – are you still attractive to them? Not just on the physical level, but also on the levels of mental, emotional and spiritual attraction. Purely on a physical level, are you wondering if you have neglected yourself, your shape, your appearance? Have you stopped being and doing sexy things? On an intimate level, what is this like now and where would you like it to be?

Looking at activities and engagements, have you developed hobbies and interests that could be obstacles and stumbling blocks to having time to spend with your significant other? Or are you both just like passing ships meeting each other on the way in or out?

Yet another aspect: you could have opted to be a stay-at-home mother and now you find your space has to be shared for the first time in years, as your partner has retired. You may feel that your freedom within the home or house is shrinking – you now have someone invading this space on a routine basis. Suddenly this is a domain that you have to share – much more so than in the past.

Connection with Your Children

Your children are adults by now as you are in this latter phase of your life. Your connection and relationship should now be from adult to adult. You released them into the world some time ago to forge their own path and carve out their relationship with the world, finding within it their unique place. The purpose in your life with them now is one more of equals and not like that of a parent with their child. Your conversations are grown-up, more like those with a friend – one step removed from the parental role, if you like. Less based on advice, criticism and monitoring, your connection is more about relationship development and growth, with advice given only when asked for.

Each of us has a unique path – parents advising their now adult offspring cannot see through the lens of their children's eyes. Certainly they cannot have an identical experience; in fact, no one can. This is because of the different thought and experiential processes each person has, making it impossible to assess the situation from the same viewpoint. So rather than get stuck in an advisory or instructive role, it is best to step back and be there if needed only. This approach is far better and leads to more harmonious relationships.

Connection with Your Grandchildren

Your role as a grandparent can be extremely rewarding. It may be a time to look at parenting skills from a more distant perspective. Indeed, it could be as a wiser, older, more mature you. You have the added benefits of reflection as you look back and may repair, if needed, issues you had with your children in a gentler way. In this grandparent role, your interaction can be freer with less responsibility and concerns on steering them into the world. There is also the benefit of being able to hand the children back after your time with them!

These interactions can be incredibly special – you can give more freely, released from the burden of being the primary guardian. With this definite space of freedom, you yourself can tap into more of you. Indulged with this freedom from responsibility, you can bring more of your essence, your loving nature to this treasured interaction. In a way it may provide you with an opportunity to be more untroubled and caring – less rigid and more flexible, the softer side of your parenting nature can come to the fore. It may also provide you with the opportunity to clear up unfinished business with your own children in the process.

These moments with your grandchildren present magical quality time which lets you express and experience the creative aspects within you – allowing opportunities to let imagination run untamed through storytelling and engaging in fun-filled games and entertainment. They also permit the opportunity to connect with and become the child within you. In certain instances, because of your upbringing, experiencing this can be very healing, bringing you into greater wholeness.

For the grandchildren this can be a treasured time and with the passage of years, fond memories will be available to them through your presence in their lives. It may also provide a time for sound values to be absorbed, which thereby influence this younger generation.

For you this can be a time for connection – pure connection without any agenda, just to BE. As you interact with these children it is great to view them as standing at the entrance of their life experience, to share in their lives through the realisation of their dreams. This may be somewhat far removed from your life with your immediate children. Your influence, perhaps, could have shaped their careers and grown from your perspective rather than through their desires and dreams. The colour of your lens could have stunted their experience of life and choice of careers.

All of these opportunities present possibilities for reflection, remorse and regret but also for repair, for clearing up any issues with your immediate children.

This time with your grandchildren provides important occasions to look into their loving eyes and see the glory and wonder, excitement, love and joy and for you to realise that they are reflecting back the essence of you at your core – your essential essence which is pure joy and love.

How brightly your light shines is directly proportional and related to your connection within. Awareness to the present moment is your key to your True Essence.

Friendships and Community Connections

As the saying goes, you are born into a family, but you choose your friends. It can take a lifetime to build and grow your circle of friends. With these friendships you have made a conscious choice to have them in your circle. In your advancing years you might be prompted to look at your friendships.

The quality of these relationships, and others too, reflects the time and importance you have attached to them. Perhaps query whether these relationships have an 'effectiveness'- rather than 'efficiency'-based quality to them. This possibly can be answered by acknowledging and appreciating the true value gained, by each of you, from that connection. Determine whether the time you have spent together was that of growing and cultivating the relationship to blossom rather than just mere ticking-the-box encounters, touching base with clock-based vigilance interspersed with texting and call answering.

Friendships have their own lifecycle, with some lasting a lifetime from childhood, others starting at school and in college years, while others still are formed over a career life or social activities and engagements in the wider community. There is a natural ebb and flow to relationships. What you bring to relationships is important. I am reminded of the Dalai Lama's quote in *The Book of Joy*:

> 'The best relationship is one in which your love for each other exceeds your need for each other.'

Friends become more important as we grow older, and we may find that there is a gentle nudge to link up with friends whom we may have lost along the way, as the busyness of life took over. True friendship does not always depend on your frequency of meeting up. It shows its presence in the generosity of support whenever needed, defined by the depth of connection, the loving and deep listening and the genuine interest available.

Deep friendships are characterised by the significance you place on them, the degree of sharing and the confidence in disclosing both heartfelt, joyous and challenging impactful issues. Such exposure and vulnerability may only be facilitated in a few of your relationships, where the level of personal disclosure is respected and honoured. At this level of a relationship, time does not have any relevance – nothing matters, only the sacred space created within this pure energy, real and true.

In the wider community, we also have influence through neighbours, institutions and organisations. At the heart of these is the individual, and the principles covered under the section of friendship also apply.

The product of our existence is developed through relationships and connections. We are and always will be connected to Source. Through the desire of Source to create further, we are 'separated' from this source of Pure Essence, Pure Consciousness, and express and experience ourselves as unique products of this energy. Our journey home is back to this Source, to rediscover our True Essence. Relationships and their connections are the principle and most important vehicle to re-establish this connection. Providing mirrors for us to see ourself or our Self, as our perfect teachers, they facilitate opportunities for us to awaken to our true nature, regardless of whether we perceive these relationships and the experiences as 'good' or 'bad'. Lessons on acceptance, acknowledgement, non-judgement, gratitude and love are woven into these interactions and are taken up as we grow into greater alignment with our True Self.

Closing comments

Relationships are gifts to us. Without them, we are isolated and we can be trapped in an ego personality. Mirrors in these relationships reflect who you are by showing you how your surroundings are treating you, including those who love you and want the absolute best for you. Your inner being is unfolding itself in experience; when you change your inner world, your exterior experience must change. Relationships just reflect what is. They can also show you what you may need to overcome within your own self. If we were to truly shift our perception and come to a greater level of awareness, we would begin to finally and truly realise that we are One. We are one with the Divine, our True Essence. We would then have the awareness that we are also one with and through all our connections and relationships. As one we are not separate, and we are not living in isolation.

In closing, in all our relationships we have the opportunity to see ourselves. Our relationships function as mirrors – reflecting us back to ourselves.

Our true nature is Love. Living in pure consciousness, love and joy is at the deepest level of our Being.

> 'Whenever you interact with people, don't be there primarily as a function or a role, but as a Field of conscious Presence.'
>
> Eckhart Tolle

Connection Questions

With the questions that follow, you have an opportunity for reflection on where you are in your life now. You may also consider what actions, if any, you may like to take following your review and response to these questions.

Keeping a regular journal may be beneficial.

When deciding on the actions needed, you may wish to put these into the SMART goal format as referenced in the Appendix. It is worthwhile to be specific about the results you wish to achieve and also to set out the tasks needed and arrange them in a logical timeframe.

Question 1

- As you consider each of your relationships and connections now, from this vantage point, how comfortable are you with each of them? Perhaps you may wish to use a scale of 1 to 10 to assess them (1 = dissatisfied and 10 = very satisfied).
    - Parents
    - Siblings
    - Significant other
    - Children
    - Grandchildren
    - Friendships and community
- If there is any unfinished business, this may be a suitable time for you to take some action now. At least consider, as a small step, to start the process.

- If you view the issue with a relationship as still raw and you are fearful of a direct intervention, you might consider writing a letter in your journal, or on a page which you then burn, using the journalling method described in the Appendix, in order to express your feelings in a private space.

- If there is any work that is specifically and solely focused on you that you have identified as needing action, it might be best to consider reviewing it in conjunction with the preceding section on the first C, Conscious Presence.

Question 2

- In your relationship with your significant other, how do you rate yourself in listening with present awareness – not only to what is spoken but also to the unspoken words and feelings?
- Present awareness involves deep listening – to take in the unspoken words and feelings. What could you do to improve this interaction between you?

Question 3

- Now that you are in your Third Act how do you feel regarding your identity and your attractiveness?

Question 4

- Does the relationship with your partner need to be re-defined?

- Changes occur during the rearing of the children, including changes in how parents relate to one another. Does this now shift again? Are adjustments needed? Has the involvement in the family unit dynamic caused friction in your relationship? How will your life together be? Will it have balance and compromise for each person's needs or will one of you dominate?

Question 5

- Have you worked out your motivational needs for yourself and also your partner?

  Note:

  There are many theories of motivational needs. Examples include:

  - Covey: These have four main elements – physical, mental, emotional/social and spiritual needs
  - Maslow's Hierarchy of Needs – The needs are depicted as a pyramid, starting at the base and progressing to the apex in the following order: physiological, safety/security, belonging (the three dependency needs); then self-esteem and self-actualisation (the two higher order/growth needs). Self-actualisation, at the deepest level, taps into Purpose and finding meaning and living from this space of knowing and expressing it to the full potential.
  - Tony Robbins' Six Motivational Needs. Robbins has defined these as:
    - Certainty: Assurance you can avoid pain and gain pleasure
    - Uncertainty/Variety: Need for new stimuli, change and the unknown
    - Significance: Feeling needed, important or special
    - Connection/Love: Closeness or union with someone/something
    - Growth: Expansion of capacity, capability or understanding
    - Contribution: A sense of service and focus on helping and serving others.

Question 6

- Of all your relationships, review which relationship stands out as the most difficult for you.
- Can you see any similarity in this for you? What is this relationship telling you about yourself? Remember: relationships hold up a mirror for us to view ourselves.

Question 7

- If there are relationships that are not serving your best interests from your Higher Self viewpoint, is there any action that you can take for the highest good of all concerned?

8

Third C: Contribution

> 'The purpose of life is to live it, to taste experience to the utmost, to reach out eagerly and without fear for newer and richer experience.'
>
> Eleanor Roosevelt

Before engaging with the subject of contribution, it is worth acknowledging that many view moving into the last phase of life as daunting. They see the stark reality that they are approaching the end-of-life phase and their only viewpoint is fixated on the fact. Their experience of life becomes gloomy. Regardless of the span of years ahead, their preferred focus is that of dread, that this is the ultimate, the final stage of life from which there is no escaping. So, it is no wonder that crossing, let alone negotiating, the Third Act from this viewpoint can be immensely challenging.

Thinking affects our health and wellbeing. Our thinking plays a key role in how we can effectively negotiate this newest phase of our life. The Appendix includes a section on Cognitive Behavioural Therapy. With awareness, we become more vigilant with our thoughts. In so doing, we have more control over our lives. When negative thoughts enter our minds and we become aware of them, we can reach for a better feeling or thought to replace the negative one. It is important to be vigilant and to consistently fill the gap created by removing that negative thought with a more life-affirming thought. Revising our mindset, we can develop neural pathways and create new norms.

The *Enchiridion* by Epictetus leaves us with something to consider:

> 'Men are disturbed not by things which happen, but by the opinion about the things ... When we are impeded, disturbed, or grieved, let us never blame others, but ourselves, that is, our opinion. It is the act of an ill-instructed man to blame others for his bad condition; it is the act of one who has begun to be instructed to lay the blame on himself; and of one whose instruction is completed, neither to blame another, nor himself.'

So now let us continue with the subject of contribution. Having shed the career, which had both its challenges and rewards, one is finally facing 'retirement'. If the Ego Self is dominant, people can cling feverishly to their identity, their roles within that career. Clocking up in the region of forty years attached to a title and its status, they now see themselves as stripped of these and hurled headlong into anonymity. It would be natural then, with this attitude, to find it difficult to adjust to this newest phase of life. They lament the passing of the previous phase and have problems with letting go.

For others, this may be viewed as an incredibly liberating time: finally freeing themselves from their commitment to supporting their family. Their work may have been less exciting or rewarding from a motivational standpoint than the previous cohort's. Nevertheless, they viewed their family commitments as important enough to continue working to this point.

Companies are increasingly offering their outgoing employees the possibility of attending retirement planning programmes. Many such programmes address the practicalities of retirement, but fail or give scant attention to the personal and emotional aspects that a person crossing this threshold can experience. Connecting with these is crucial to live life with passion, power, and purpose. Difficult as this stage can be for that individual, it can and often is coupled with the partner meeting an equal challenge.

In coaching clients through this phase of life and seeing certain themes emerge, I felt drawn to designing a programme for both men and women to negotiate this transition successfully. 'Reignite: The Retirement Ready Programme' was born: the inner journey to negotiate this phase of life using seven keys. The overriding message is that you are a unique being with gifts and talents. The key to life is to ENJOY it. This is a choice, with the journey being more important than the destination. As R.L. Stevenson says:

'... to travel hopefully is a better thing than to arrive ...'

Contribution is a fascinating subject, particularly so as our lifespan has expanded by thirty years from that of our great-grandparents. As stated earlier, these additional years can be considered as another full phase of adulthood, a second phase of adulthood. With this sizeable amount of time, hopefully, we can leave our unique mark on the world. We can take the opportunity presented in our Third Act to influence society and the world by making individual and collective contributions.

But firstly, and more importantly, this period presents time for you to focus on the most important person in your life, YOU. You as a unique human being, and you as a powerful woman. So, it is worth investing time to explore who you really are, at this mid-life stage, having accumulated a wealth of experience and a few grey hairs along the way, if you are open to admit it. You still have many years left. Despite the media and society at large, which in my view is becoming an ever-increasingly 'ageist' society, you are not 'past it'. Connect to your spirit, find your True Self, which is always present within you. Enjoy living each day from your Authentic Self.

Make up your mind to honour and celebrate yourself as you embrace this gift and stage of life: thrive in your Third Act.

> 'The deepest secret is that life is not a process of discovery, but a process of creation.'
> *Conversations with God*, Book 1, Neale Donald Walsch

This is an ideal time for you to grow and evolve into the greatest expression of yourself to date. Finding purpose is a crucial element to living a fulfilled and meaningful life. Developing your unique expression through your gifts and talents and sharing these within your world, your community. You light your light and joyfully express yourself.

So, you may well ask: how does one find one's purpose? Getting to know yourself is the obvious starting point. Find out what brings meaning and joy to your life. What is important to you? What values do you cherish? How would you like to express yourself in the world? Finding quiet time in nature, meditating or journaling can support this type of enquiry. Also, think about how you can be of service to others rather than just focusing on yourself. Marry this with what you love doing and what brings you joy. Doing something that you are passionate about and something that is needed in the world brings you into greater alignment with your Self.

Eleanor Roosevelt puts this rather nicely in the quote at the beginning of this section.

The Third Act is also a time to influence society and the world – to make significant inroads with our individual and collective contributions and to serve others. I strongly believe that we really have a chance to make a difference for future generations by leaving this world in a better, richer place. I am reminded of Ralph Waldo Emerson's poem on success:

> 'To laugh often and much;
> To win the respect of intelligent people and the affection of children;
> To earn the appreciation of honest critics and endure the betrayal of false friends;
> To appreciate beauty,
> To find the best in others;

> To leave the world a bit better, whether by a healthy child, a garden patch, or a redeemed social condition;
> To know even one life has breathed easier because you have lived
> This is to have succeeded.'

These additional years are not just about filling in the time with endless activity for activity's sake. We have been given this time for a good reason. We came into this lifetime at this time, with the world in a very turbulent place, a challenging time for the earth and its people. What is our part to play in the greater scheme of things? What are we being called to do?

Begin by taking a step back to conduct a review, a stock-taking of your life to date.

Through this review exercise we can reclaim things that were important to us in earlier years, which we may have cast aside for valid reasons at the time. We can reassess our values and priorities as we see them now, making the necessary adjustments. We can redefine who we are. We can reconnect with our passion and creativity.

Our true nature is pure joy and love. Living this path daily in isolation is great, but in reality, most of us live in a world connected with others. Oftentimes, and particularly in the Third Act, strange things happen. We know relationships do not always run smoothly and they may come into sharp focus within this review, highlighting issues that may now need to be addressed as you move forward. These relationships could be with family or friends, or it could be the one with a significant other. A pragmatic approach for the latter would be to develop your Self and then support, loving the other and allowing them to follow their own specific path, their own journey.

As a couple, the legacy of your relationship is the harmony developed and nurtured between you, and the space provided within the relationship for the unfoldment of each partner's unique and individual legacy. The bond of love in the united relationship flourishes, emanating onwards with ripple effects on the wider family unit and community. With the couple possibly unaware of the end result, this loving influence reaches out, affecting others, presenting a model of higher life and possibilities for others.

In your other relationships, it is necessary to approach them also with love. Clear up issues from your own standpoint and with the other party, if possible, and move forward from this point onwards with greater depth in the relationship. Sometimes, relationships cannot be repaired. The key point here is that you have done what you can. Others may not be able to do so for whatever reasons. In fact, often, with deep work done on yourself, an unintended consequence may be that this causes problems for the other person, with the unfortunate result of projection and blame for unresolved issues and wounds from the past. Dealing with such a scenario is difficult and may require a parting of the ways, however painful. Be aware, however, that these people possibly are your best teachers, and your path is to stay on course to develop more into your Authentic Self – the True Self. The biggest decision to make is to continue to see through the eyes of love. Act with integrity and conviction – following the path of compassion and reaching for higher levels of conscious awareness.

Yet another aspect of this review exercise is that it could also throw up some feelings of remorse, regarding relationships or actions taken or not taken in business or personal life. It would be unwise to use this as a stick to beat yourself with. Rather, adopt the viewpoint that this is an opportunity to make amends and learn from the experience.

By going back and revisiting these and other painful memories, you can clear up these issues by doing the work necessary rather than contaminate more years. It means you can finally lay down the burden you have been carrying all these years and move forward freely.

It is also worth mentioning that sometimes, in moving too quickly from one project to another, we overlook celebration. We need to rejoice and recognise our strengths and achievements. We may indeed wish to reclaim these and carry them through to the next phase of our life.

This review of your life gives you the opportunity for a new signature and meaning to your life. You have the freedom of choice.

The sacred gift of these additional years is our opportunity to develop into wholeness. A time for us to become wise, to demonstrate and pass on wisdom. Finally, this time presents us with the greatest gift of all: to become, experience and live our lives as our Authentic Self. A time to live and enjoy life, giving full expression to our unique divinity – living and experiencing Who We Really Are, centred in our Authentic Self.

Living from this Authentic Self, we experience life more wholly, we are more confident, dropping our anxiety and worry, we achieve more in a relaxed way, and we interact with others in more meaningful, considerate and loving ways.

Living from this space means that we continue to grow and evolve. We are actively engaged with the higher motivational needs not only for growth for ourselves, but also those for service to others and for contribution. We are on a mission to find our way back to our true home – to merge with Divine Consciousness. Occasionally, we may forget that we were always connected to it: there is no separation and there never was. It is for us a journey to reconnect, to remember Who We Truly Are.

In this phase we are more attuned to our inner guidance. We are clearer on the purpose and meaning of our lives and why we are here. We have been given an opportunity to lead the way, to be an example, and to hold the light for future generations. We stand at the bridge between past generations and future generations to come. Increasingly, we are coming to realise the illusion that we and our forebears lived in.

We now have the knowledge and possibility to stand up and take our rightful place. We are, in a way, 'Light Bearers', Warriors of the Light. We live at an interesting time in history. Let your light shine.

The 'Divine Feminine' concept is receiving increasing attention. It is a topic that may not be understood by some. This can result in fear arising, even if they have not explored this topic. For this reason, I have decided to briefly discuss this topic. Before I begin, let me dispel the notion that this is pitting women against men.

As mentioned already in Chapter 6, First C, the Divine Feminine concept posits that within each of us, and in the world at large, there are energies which are complementary, i.e. masculine and feminine energies. The Divine Feminine is the feminine aspect of the divine power that connects all of Earth together. Within each of us, regardless of how we present, this goddess energy exists. This Divine Feminine energy is seen in many cultures – Isis (Egyptian), Aphrodite (Greek) and Shakti (Hindu) to name but a few. The Divine Feminine refers to the spiritual aspect of what it is to be human. This feminine energy within and around us has been overshadowed on a societal level by the masculine energies. The results of this masculine energy dominance are evidenced in war, violence, abuse of power, greed and corruption. The time has now come for these energies to become balanced.

In a recent interview with Dermot Morris on the *Brendan O'Connor Show* on 9 October 2022, this theme was echoed. For 1 million years humans lived in small communities of about 80 to 100 people, with the female central to these. The male was peripheral. He went hunting, developing specialised tasks as the risk-taker, and killing and bringing back the prey for the tribe. Moving on through the years, he moved from agriculture into towns and cities. Here males hunted down business contracts and deals. From that point onwards, men unfairly dominated women. Morris mentioned that it was only in the last century that women started to reclaim their ancient birthright, in which they were central and organised everything – so now there is a movement to rebalance the energies.

The qualities associated with the Divine Feminine include abundance, being (rather than doing), compassion, creativity, emotion, growth, intuition, joy, love, nurturing, openness, vulnerability and sensitivity. This feminine power is more internal and receptive. Through meditation as an example of a personal journey inwards, we can connect to our True Self. On the other hand, masculine energy flows outward; it is external and associated more with the qualities of doing and actively asserting power. So, by going inward, we can discover our True Self and awaken the Divine Feminine, to reach wholeness through union by rebalancing the male and female energies. We need to restore harmony and peace within us as individuals. In doing so, we can experience the True Self and live a joyful and meaningful life. We can then reflect this out into the world.

As we connect with what gives us joy in our lives, we can begin to think about setting goals on projects for which we are passionate. When we consider that we can develop, and even share our passion and gifts with a wider audience, we can decide that there are a number of goals to commit to paper. It may be helpful to remember the following:

- The past does not determine the future.
- Procrastination is the enemy. So, start small and then build momentum. Having a vision and setting goals can be revisited regularly.
- Be mindful that we need to dwell more in present awareness.

In this respect, and some people find this a tricky thing to grasp, when setting goals, it is done in the present moment. We can use the SMART concept to develop goals. Refer to the Appendix for the details on this.

All actions that we take are undertaken in a present moment in time. Therefore, we can be present in the moment when performing the actions and activities which support a given goal. The present is the only place we have – the past is gone and the future has yet to unfold, and when it does it will be in the present moment.

To add a further point, consider the law of attraction. Simply put, it is about attracting to ourselves that which is similar to the quality of thoughts and feelings that we hold. When goal setting to successfully attract what you desire, it is necessary to do this from the silence of pure awareness. In this state of consciousness your desire will be in accord with all of nature, it will have the power and intelligence of the cosmos behind it. Your true nature is love, joy and wisdom. When you experience and know this, you will attract love, joy and wisdom into your life.

The idea of finding joy may be still a somewhat abstract concept, despite all that has been mentioned up to now about tapping into what gives you joy. The discussion on finding joy has so far been outward-focused. So, I would like to develop this theme a bit further and share some words from my recent re-reading of *The Book of Joy*, by His Holiness the Dalai Lama and Archbishop Desmond Tutu with Douglas Abrams, in particular the section 'Days 4 and 5: The Eight Pillars of Joy'. Joy and happiness have been described as by-products of qualities (the eight pillars) of the mind and heart that we need 'to cultivate to catch the bus'. Mental immunity can be improved by reducing fear, anger and other obstacles. However, as described in this book, the Dalai Lama explained that these qualities need to be coupled with filling the mind and heart with positive thoughts and feelings.

The distillation from the discussions of the Dalai Lama and Desmond Tutu converged on eight pillars of joy. Four of these were mind-based qualities: perspective, humility, humour and acceptance. The remaining four qualities, which related to the heart, were: forgiveness, gratitude, compassion and generosity.

> 'We create most of our suffering, so we should be able to create more joy.'
>
> Dalai Lama

In closing, our contribution to community, our world, younger generations and those yet to come is the celebration of our uniqueness in living from our Authentic Self. From this solid place of the Authentic Self, we can live more wholly, live from a place of love and joy. Wayne Dyer has a wonderful saying:

> 'When you dance, your purpose is not to get to a certain place on the floor. It is to enjoy each step along the way.'

We can embrace life, living consciously in the present moment as Wise Women: strong and confident, embracing our gifts and talents centred in Love and Joy, in Knowing Who We Really Are at the core of our Being.

So, in viewing contribution, we need to firstly focus on developing and growing ourselves and giving to ourselves. Having filled up the well within us, we can live from a place of love and joy, shine forth our light, and share with the world.

> 'Success is not a function of the size of your title but the richness of your contribution.'
>
> Robin Sharma

Contribution Questions

With the questions that follow, you have an opportunity for reflection on where you are in your life now. You may also consider what actions, if any, you may like to take following your review and response to these questions.

Keeping a regular journal may be beneficial.

When deciding on the actions needed, you may wish to put these into the SMART goal format as referenced in the Appendix. It is worthwhile to be specific about the results you wish to achieve and also to set out the tasks needed and arrange them in a logical timeframe.

Question 1

- Have you ever wondered what your life is really about? What is it that you are supposed to do? What are your initial thoughts on this?

Question 2

Reflection – The Wise Woman

- The phase of the Third Act of your life inevitably means that you have accumulated a lot of life experience to date. This phase can earn you the title 'Wise Woman'.
- From all your life experience, reflect now and consider which of these experiences have made you whole and wise. Describe three of these.

Question 3

- Using the information gleaned from Question 2, how could your experiences be drawn upon to help others at this time? Itemise three if you can. Perhaps these can be put into SMART goal format. Refer to the Appendix for further information.

Question 4

Values

- Review your answers to Question 1 of Chapter 6 (First C: Conscious Presence) on your values. Are you still satisfied that these are the values important to you? Are there any values you wish to delete from or add to the list?
- Select the top five from your list. Describe why these values are so important to you.
- Your values are ones consciously chosen by you. You have no reason to adopt another's values and take them on unless you resonate with these values today. This is your life and only you are the author of your life.

Question 5

- From the discussion on the eight pillars to joy (four of the mind (Perspective, Humility, Humour, Acceptance) and four of the heart (Forgiveness, Gratitude, Compassion, Generosity)), measure how satisfied you are in yourself with each of these on a scale of 1 to 10 (1 = dissatisfied and 10 = extremely satisfied).
- Consider working on a few of the ones you are less satisfied with, say over the next 18 months.
- You could set these in SMART goal format. You may even like to journal about your progress with these.

PART III

Ann's Story: Thoughts and Interactions with the 3 Cs

9

Introduction

March 2019 – something had been gently nudging me for the last 24 months to draft a book on women, for women. During the final stages of editing my first book, CARE of Leadership (March 2017), I had made a commitment to myself to continue to engage in writing. Some months later, during a meditation while holidaying in Lanzarote, I had further clarity on the contents for this book. The structure would be simple, centring on the '3 Cs': the associated words 'conscious presence', 'connection' and 'contribution'. I quickly jotted them down in my journal lest they take off into the ether.

True to my nature of not doing things by halves, I started dabbling with another project of interest, one that focused on 'retirement'. I personally do not believe I will ever really retire; my desire is to continue working in the personal development field with programmes, seminars, books and coaching services. Since 2017 my doctors had been urging me to slow down and had suggested that I should consider retiring.

This notion certainly was pressing buttons for me, and ones that left me feeling uncomfortable. I was, after all, still alive, passionate about my work as a human development consultant, on a personal mission with the vision to evolve – developing my gifts and talents to the fullest and in doing so helping others awaken to realising their dreams and goals. So, the idea of 'REIGNITE', a book on living a fulfilling Third

Act, started to take root. I like working with acronyms – REIGNITE was going to encompass the following concepts:

- 'RE' contained both positive and negative themes. Review, Reassess, Recreate, Redefine, Reclaim, Rejoice and Relax formed one group, and the other included Regret, Remorse and Reject.
- 'I' related to Identity and how an individual sees themselves once they are retired.
- 'G' addressed Goals and vision.
- 'N' introduced the subject matter of Negative thoughts and their impact.
- 'I' discussed the Integration of the newest, best version of oneself, having eliminated interfering negative thoughts.
- 'T' spoke about Taking action to realise the vision and goals previously set.
- 'E' pulled the preceding themes together and looked at Embracing and Enjoying life.

The two themes of women in their power and the subject of retirement were inter-related. Initially this was a source of confusion for me: should they be rolled together as a single project, or should I untangle them and have two distinct projects? Clarity finally dawned: the retirement programme (as in REIGNITE) was equally relevant to both men and women. The projects did not need to be interwoven. The power of women could be a stand-alone project, presented as a book, while REIGNITE would be a training programme/seminar for both men and women. This appeared to be the obvious solution and I settled on this approach as having two distinct projects which nicely encompassed my intended goals.

For the power of women particularly, as an older cohort of society, perhaps my efforts through my projects could in some way provide guidance and play a role in nurturing for generations to come. The strength and importance of women in society as referenced through the ages in Irish mythology should be acknowledged. Further, I believe that Ireland is, at its heart, a matriarchal society. A changing future for

Ireland greatly needs the nurturing, caring, supportive, creative and intuitive gifts which women naturally bestow.

I had a few hazy brushstrokes for the book – the first two of the 3 Cs and a concrete subject for the third C, 'contribution'. But despite this, ideas were not flowing. There was a block in my creative pipeline. I realised after some time that this was in reality mirroring my own struggles at figuring out what my contribution was.

My business set-up in 2001 offered Quality Consultancy as one strand and Organisation and Personal Development as the other, delivered through training programmes and coaching. In 2018, I decided to focus solely on training and development. The Covid-19 environment that followed over the next couple of years resulted in economic uncertainty for a sizeable number of businesses. This had a direct knock-on effect on training and development businesses, and mine was no exception. 'Staying afloat' was the adopted mantra for many businesses. Investment in training and development took a 'back seat' as companies deemed it 'non-essential'.

This time afforded an opportunity for reflection. What surfaced over this time was that I was being pulled off course personally with the programmes that I was still delivering to a reduced client base. I felt that continuing to deliver my original training offerings was holding me back from a deeper spiritual path. This was a source of disharmony for me, particularly if it were to continue.

For my own spiritual journey and growth, I needed to develop offerings more closely aligned to my life's purpose. These would include programmes with the focus on an inner journey to the realisation of the Self and living from this place. These programmes would support participants to awaken to their own uniqueness, and connect and express their gifts and talents. I was unwaveringly passionate about making a contribution in this field. I acknowledged this turnabout, and that I needed to listen to what was calling me.

The first decision I made was to stop doing anything that did not make me feel good. It was an amazing revelation to me to just do things that were joyful to me. Looking back on this now it seems so easy, but it was hard for me. I had, after all, come from the conditioned thinking that consistent, demanding work, effort and persistence would win out and reach a successful conclusion. Something deep, deep down inside of me was stopping me. My body was tired, my actions were slower, and things were stagnant. Urgent change was needed. This required taking a different approach. I had to stop swimming against the flow.

So, changing and embarking on this new direction would lead to greater fulfilment for me, knowing that I would be living more in alignment with my life purpose in serving others. I knew felt more peaceful with this decision.

My love for art was rekindled over ten years ago. I had joined an art class, promising myself that I would develop this talent. I painted with great enthusiasm and found I was more relaxed with this creative expression of myself. At present, I'm not attending any regular classes. My painting continues, tapping into joyous states, lost in the moment with my canvas and brush. Having dropped my perfectionist art critic, my love affair with art is drawing me deeper into Who I Really Am. Art was the key to me unlocking and allowing myself to enter joyful states.

Art also acted as the catalyst to take a serious look at my hectic running and doing, making sure that others in my circle were alright. I had possibly spent too much time in this mode and thereby overextended myself as a result. I needed first to see what was fuelling this, then create a better balance here, one which would nurture me more, whilst still connecting with those who were important to me.

I slowly began to focus on me. I would be fine with the decision in stepping back from pharma projects and just continue to deliver whatever management and personal developments programmes were requested, at least for the short term. This arrangement would also be acceptable to me from a financial perspective.

I felt that I was now being asked to move in a new direction; other doors were now coming into my view. These doors would take me on a journey into my Third Act. This would be and is now a new adventure for me, one where my own story is part of that unfoldment. It is also part of my gift to other people on that journey too. My offering now comes from a place of contribution. Helping and supporting others through this phase, the Third Act. This, coupled with a particular focus on women, was going to be my calling. This was going to separate me from my company as I knew it, setting me on a new and deeper path, more in alignment with my soul purpose. I was now clear for the first time in a long while. No longer would I be striving to fit my contribution into the slot of having to meet business and financial targets and pushing to make that happen.

For me now, my contribution is to have books, programmes and seminars available: *Power of W: Women Thriving in Their Third Act* (book) and REIGNITE: the Retirement Ready Programme about Living a Fulfilled Third Act. These initial offerings, I feel, are coming from a pure, heartfelt space and one where I am more centred in my Authentic Self, more in alignment with my true essence.

I am living in my Third Act now. In the years leading up to the publication of this book, I faced many challenges in my personal life and closest relationships. Finding the higher meaning in these events is now clear. Processing these has given me deeper insights. I am now truly integrating all my life to date into this third phase, that of the 'Crone' or 'Wise Woman', and living from this place more as my Authentic Self and connection to my core essence.

The resolution of the struggle I experienced can be summed up in a journal entry over this time: *' all it took was to be in darkness and be present to me – my I Am Self.'*

In closing, I am of the late 60s vintage, and I hope that I will still engage with activities and projects that both excite me and draw on my talents and gifts for all the remaining years of my life here.

Through workshops and seminars, I experience more of living in the present moment, being aware, and a deep sense of connection with my true essence.

Art has been my anchor, it has brought me back to my Self and states of joy. I continue to breathe, express and live joyfully in this connection.

My books have also provided me with an avenue to connect to my Self. *CARE of Leadership* (2017) was my first offering as an author.

It only lightly touched on our core essence. This light approach was adopted due to the fact that the audience for this book was predominantly business-oriented. However, *Power of W: Women Thriving in Their Third Act* has moved me more deeply towards discussing who we really are, our True Self and our connection with pure consciousness. This is the field of infinite possibilities, open to all to connect with. In so doing we can manifest through experience and express the uniqueness of our Being, our expression of divinity.

More important for me is that I engage with life through activities which bring me to joyful states, and that my engagement with people adds to and increases their level of joy.

I am now in greater alignment with my True Self. 'Surrendering to what is' has been one of the hardest and yet one of the most rewarding lessons I have learned. Intellectually, it was easy to understand but practically – well that was a different matter entirely. I continue to grow deeper roots with my surrender process.

In the sections that follow I have included some extracts from journal writings, including those on the more recent Caminos undertaken in 2018 and 2022 and the immediate weeks which followed.

These journal entries represent my engagement with the central themes in *Power of W: Women Thriving in Their Third Act*: The 3 Cs – Conscious Presence, Connection and Contribution. These have been woven into my current thoughts on these themes.

10

First C: Thoughts on Interacting with Conscious Presence

'Life is a series of natural and spontaneous changes. Don't resist them; that only creates sorrow. Let reality be reality. Let things flow naturally forward in whatever way they like.'

Lao Tzu

2018 – A SELECTION OF EXTRACTS FROM JOURNAL ENTRIES

The question I have for myself is 'Why is it taking so long to get the impetus to start drafting the book on the Power of W: Women Thriving in Their Third Act?' I would like to start and write this now but there is something holding me back. There is still fear there; fear that I will not be accepted as a writer in this very specific aspect of personal development, considering that this is a new departure for me.

Also, I am querying both what I want to say for the first 'C' – 'Conscious Presence', and whether I should link this to my heritage of having roots in the Celtic and Druidic past. In reading around this subject, and also intuitively, I know that the women from these ages past were powerful. I would dearly love to tune in and connect with the flow of this female ancestral energy to which I feel drawn. It appears to be similar to the energies that I experienced on my visits to Glastonbury (UK) many years past. Both ancient Ireland and Glastonbury energies seem to be calling me. I would really like to get more in tune and in flow with them.

The ancient woman, the Celtic druidic woman, remained detached for part of her life. Part of each day was devoted to her Self. The preservation of Self and reconnection with Self needed to be maintained as part of a ritual: the ritual of Wise Women. This did not mean that they were disconnected from community, husband or family. But it clearly means that, in a sacred time, this ritual was observed to connect with all aspects of SELF.

This going within involved connecting to the inner voice – the voice of ultimate guidance – the pure sweet voice which can only be heard in quiet times: in nature, the whistling of the wind, the trees, bark, branches, leaves – delivering their messages and calling to me.

To finish this journal entries section, particularly that of the 'fear' voiced in the opening paragraph as to whether I would be accepted as a writer in this field of personal development, I am reminded that as human beings we are all equal and of equal value. Further, it is good to remember the source from which our gifts and talents arise. Archbishop Tutu puts this theme rather nicely: 'God uses each of us in our own way, and even if you are not the best one, you may be the one who is needed or the one who is there.'

Stepping out, doing something unfamiliar is challenging. So, fear is not unexpected. However, the inner calling is stronger and bringing me into greater alignment with Self.

* * *

The ocean and its majestic waves thundering to the shore relentlessly are showing their mighty power. A reminder to me of my power within. A reminder too for conscious presence to call it forth, and to hush the mind full of thoughts and empty these and let things unfold. To be alive to my connections, my husband, and to extend this to the people in my circle. A reminder to be alive and present to the hollow curl of the waves: to feel their vibrations to the core of my being; to bring me back to me. To Be, to be present to my Self.

To be with all there is – the I Am. This is the soulful connection that I desire: this is my only true connection. With its presence and me connected I feel truly alive again. Alive and yet still. Alive and present to the gifts that unfold. Alive to my connections and my husband in this life. Alive and present to the people of my circle. Alive and present to the community beyond me.

The desire for the I Am is deep and for me this embracing connection is ME – this is the True Me. There is no separation. It is always present. Thinking 'small' would bereft me of my rightful place. Self-beggared, would be the result if I were to deprive myself of the regular practice of tuning in and tapping into this greater part of me. I Am with it now – I am true to this space, and I am calling it forth to be with me: alive and living from this space – a Divine space that I rightfully connect to and embrace. This is the REAL ME – alive, vibrant, abundant, with loving kindness that imbues all my life – my life as Ann; my life with my husband; my life with friends, family, and community. A life which is now filled, lived fully, and is fulfilling, a life of freedom.

FREEDOM

Free in this Home within me – confident, secure, and centred.

* * *

The following extract from the journal includes a note for the readers of my potential next book.

You, dear reader, are given the opportunity to know yourself – this involves setting some time aside each day, as part of your day, to be with you. To connect with the deeper part of you which can only be truly heard in quiet moments. Freedom from the clutter is needed: carve out some time during the day, each day, to make a lovely ritual to connect with your Self. This ritual can take many forms – being in nature, quiet moments in meditation or with your eyes open, bringing you into stillness – presence. In these moments, wonderous gifts are there for you. The presence of Self; your true presentation of you – the 'I AM' – the unique and powerful. This is your time in this sacred space to draw and be nourished from it. By calling it forth more, this inner presence becomes the greater part of your outer daily presence. This great, powerful you, which stands tall and confident, standing present in your place in the world, your world.

* * *

This state, which is represented by flow, is the connection and calling forth of WHO I really AM, and who I am unveiling and becoming – this is a love story and dance with my I AM.

I am making my journey and hope it could also to be an encouraging lead for all those searching for this superb sacred connection – to the still small voice, to call it forth more frequently and to be more BEING in its presence.

In writing these words I feel this deep connectedness

This powerful presence that is I AM. This is Who I really AM.

The writing of this first C, Conscious Presence, is the commitment to my wholeness without which I would be operating in the world with a lesser, weaker presence.

Drawing forth this deeper Self brings a wisdom and wealth to the whole of life: a life made of many parts. From our conscious connection we can bring forth our True Self and shine our light as we stand in Conscious Presence.

* * *

2022 – A SELECTION OF EXTRACTS FROM JOURNAL ENTRIES

April 2022 was the first Camino I undertook solo.

I enjoyed this solitude and the opportunity of being in communion with Self. The Sarria to Portomarin segment presented several whispers needing to reach my ears. This way progressed with only a few pilgrims walking this stretch so early this particular morning. I first encountered the babbling brook, which spoke of being flexible and moving with the flow. As I continued the trail, with each step connecting more consciously with the ground, my stick absorbed the whisper to 'take the path of least resistance', a message badly needed for my life. As I progressed through the kilometres of this day, with nature seeping into my being, the clear message landed: 'Stop doing when you are not having fun.' This was as profound as it was simple. I needed to hear and heed this one. Life had become all too serious. Nearing the end of the journey for today, I was counting the kilometres left. This was an effort to motivate and propel me forward as I was feeling the tiredness in my legs. I was at my limit, my legs were aching badly as I continued to press on. The message received was two-fold: 'Be mindful of taking care of the body. It is needed to encase the soul' and 'Watch out for Being as opposed to Doing'.

The final whisper of the day was 'Joy is your highest calling and anything that lessens this for you needs to end. So, when you become aware of non-joyful states, you need to stop, take a breath, and bring yourself back to the present moment. This is your exercise for the remainder of the Camino. Got it? Get it. Only playing with you now. You know I love you. Stay well and joyful.'

Now, as I reflect on that day, I am reminded of a key paradox in Buddhism which resonated with me on a pattern I had with goal setting. The essence of the teaching was that while goals are needed for growth and development, it is important not to get overly attached to these goal aspirations. Putting it another way, the commitment to the goal should not be contingent on our ability to attain it. We need to loosen our grip, and not hold to rigid assumptions which we have created about how we must achieve our goals.

* * *

My conscious steps allowed me to absorb nature around me. It presented some great photos. Occasionally, I had the welcome interruptions from fellow pilgrims. Today I received a nugget of inspiration supporting my intention when I sat in the cathedral, the day before I start my Camino. The intention set was to get a very clear direction on my life purpose. This specific message was to combine my art and the potential third book that I had earmarked the previous year into a different project. In the cathedral I also asked that the frustration surrounding the stagnation of getting my second book finished would cease shortly. The whisper I received was that everything would flow more freely once I had completed three paintings from this current Camino.

Once back at my home base, the easel was quickly located and that was the first stimulus to get reconnected to my writings. Flicking through the gallery of photos taken on the most recent Camino, the first one was easy to select. Even now as I commit these words to paper, I have a vivid memory of the subject. It was a tree that was struck by lightning and had its centre ripped open (see page 107). This image to me was that of an open heart. As I looked at this photo, I was transported back to that day on the Camino, clearly remembering the message that was whispered to me as I stopped and gazed at this tree.

'Continue to keep your heart fully open.'

The tree itself was dead. Yet, its presence was powerful. Some ivy had taken root and was growing on the trunk. Two limbs of branches stretching upwards to the skyline. There was also a further message from this tree:

'Acceptance and surrender.'

This was powerful. Even as I type these words it is chilling. I now get the full impact of this message, as I believe it related to the events yet to unfold in July 2022, some months after this Camino. I am also reminded, and also now know experientially that joy requires the essential ingredient of an open heart, even, and possibly especially, in the face of life's challenges. With an open heart we can feel our own pain (and that of another). Paradoxically, we are also able to experience more joy.

The next painting was going to be of a silver birch – its photo captured on an early morning start on my trail (page 108).

This silver birch whose truncated branch seemed to whisper to me:

'Be Still and Listen.'

The final painting subject was the stepping-stones through a forest that had a small river pool on the track (page 109). I knew this particular spot from previous Caminos I had undertaken.

All three paintings were completed within a month. The last one, I believe, is the best, even though I had not selected this particular photo initially. The message of the photo and the subsequent painting was:

'Move forward, take the stepping-stones presented and avoid the apparently slow moving, almost stagnant waters.'

Through these painting and the whispers I am reminded that life is not always easy. It is wise to accept reality and know that even it too will pass. We cannot deny reality. With acceptance the door for change opens to us. It allows us to move into joyful states.

I decided to select another photo, with a related theme of the three paintings already completed – that of going with the flow. This was eventually painted in November 2022 and represented the whispering of

'moving forward to a bright unknown path'.

* * *

I was drawn to undertake a second Camino in 2022. This one was from Santiago de Compostela to Finisterre, which I completed in September that year.

I had previously driven through this part of Galicia but had not walked it until now. My intention in the cathedral at Santiago, before I turned my back to it, was that my writing would be at an advanced stage at the end of this Camino.

I had received answers on the previous Camino to the main projects with which I needed to engage. My writing in my journal entries on this latest Camino as it happened were minimal, but the whisperings from the path were many. They varied from meetings with fellow pilgrims and others and swimming in the ocean on beaches near Finisterre to several visits over a number of days to the lighthouse at the cliff edge of Finisterre. These are some of the whispers:

'Linear time is false time. So, stop worrying about this – there is infinite time in the present moment.'

'Slow the pace down. Be at one with nature. You will feel and be in your essence when you connect with nature all around you.'

'Live life in the moment as it flows to you.'

'Your life is filled with infinite possibilities. Open your arms and embrace them.'

'How many years of life do you think you have to live ...'

'You hold the key to happiness in your life.'

'Let no one steal this key from you.'

The messages here were clear and the theme from earlier in the year echoed in this more recent Camino. I am reminded once again of the acceptance of reality. This reduces stresses, which are caused when we react to circumstances which life presents rather than bravely accept them. There is no point in arguing with reality.

Yet another nugget of wisdom for me was the final realisation that it is impossible to experience joy when we deny or resist reality.

This message was reinforced in my readings of *The Book of Joy* and the realisation that living in joy does not mean that life will be free of pain. It also spoke to the need of accepting reality and seeing if 'we can turn this into something positive' .

In the late afternoon of 21 September 2022, I arrived in Ireland. Within 24 hours I had a strong impulse to review the draft of *Power of W*, which had remained untouched for over two years. Each day from that point onwards I reviewed what I had previously written and continued to add sections until the complete first draft of the manuscript was ready on 21 October, just 24 hours before I would set out for Portugal. Yes, time is a changing thing!

'Yesterday I was clever, so I wanted to change the world. Today I am wise, so I am changing myself.'

Rumi

Tree struck by lightning, like an open heart

Silver birch

Forest path with stepping stones

11

Second C: Thoughts on Interacting with Connection

'A friend is one to whom one may pour out the contents of one's heart, chaff and grain together, knowing that gentle hands will take and sift it, keep what is worth keeping, and with a breath of kindness, blow the rest away.'

George Eliot

2018 – A SELECTION OF EXTRACTS FROM JOURNAL ENTRIES

Contemplating Connection as I stood on a beach, my attention was drawn to a shell. What follows are the streams of thoughts, feelings and questions that surfaced for me on this November day shortly after daybreak on this beach – a peaceful and undisturbed setting.

- *What is our shell like and what is our core like?*
- *Are we talking about the shell as the core or is it an outer part of us?*
- *Where does our True Core reside?*

These, I guess, are some interesting questions worth exploring. My True Self resides within me and is the constant and never-changing aspect of Who I Really Am. To get to this level, digging deep is necessary to connect into this essence – which is pure Love and Joy. So, this is who we really are at our core. We are an aspect of Divinity – Love and Joy. We are all connected, we are all divinity. 'Namaste', the Indian greeting and blessing (Sanskrit), echoes this message. Namaste means 'The divine light in me bows to the divine light within you'. We are honouring the place in each other where the entire universe dwells.

Through the meaning in this blessing, we can become far more conscious of our connectedness to everyone and everything.

A shell as a word implies a structure, our outer structure, and it may not always reflect this inner aspect of us. It may not embody our true nature and as a result may not reflect the highest aspect of us. Shells could be likened to personality and something that we have put in place and designed for ourselves, for us to manage in our world. Others, too, have this same operating mechanism.

So, our personalities are this shell and the mechanism by which we interact with our environment. Personality is our coping mechanism, our protective shell. Is this personality real? Yes, it is real, but it is not the real You.

This in turn leads to a deeper question relating to what we project into the world as a whole, into our world and to those within our circle. The connections we have with each of these people is different. The degree and the quality of these interactions each can be varied and unique perhaps. The meaning and value we hold for each may be different, as indeed is our motivation for interactions. So, exploring how we think and feel about these connections is important. A big question for me is how I show up for each of these interactions – with my significant other, family, friends, work colleagues, community and the greater world.

In these interactions there is congruence between what is projected outwards and our shell and, more importantly, congruence between that shell and the True Self at our core; the essence of who we are becoming, who we wish to align with.

We are not islands and therefore we need to connect with others. So, what are we trying to do in each of the connections, the interactions with the various individuals in our life? Are we happy in these varied relationships in our life? More importantly, how do we show up in these relationships? Are they consistent with our truth?

Do we feel better in the moment with the interaction in which we are engaged? If we feel that the answer is no, maybe we should explore what we could have done better to enhance that interaction – in either our thoughts, words, or deeds. Were we truly present for this interaction? Was there a difference between the way we were feeling during the interaction and the feeling after that engagement?

It may be beneficial at this point to view all the relationships within our life. To start to take stock of where we are right now and where we desire to be. Yes, it is up to us, not the other, to change and influence the relationship from our part. We cannot change another, only ourselves. We may not necessarily like to hear that it is up to us to make the improvements. We can be the best ingredient in the relationship, we can influence the process; however, we cannot determine the outcome – we do not have control over this aspect. There are others in the equation over whose response to our input and ensuing actions we have no control.

However, we do owe it to ourselves to act from the highest possible stance, to show up in the best possible way we can, in the moment. If we do not like the choice we made in a particular moment, we have the potential and choice to change our actions and choose something better to enhance our inputs to the interactive engagement. To choose and reach for something higher that is more in alignment with our essential nature. This alone will make us feel better in the process and tap into what we truly desire.

Much later, when revisiting my resources on a 21-day meditation through *Miraculous Relationships* by Deepak Chopra and Oprah Winfrey, I was reminded that every one of us wants to be seen, heard and understood. So, when listening to another we need to engage in deep listening. Chopra recommends connecting on the level of being and hearing the other with your heart. This type of listening is not just to the words said, but also to what is not said and the feelings behind these. Only by connecting on a heart-to-heart level are you listening with complete awareness.

> 'Have a big enough heart to love unconditionally, and a broad enough mind to embrace the differences that make each of us unique.'
>
> D.B. Harrop

12

Third C: Thoughts on Interacting with Contribution

> 'You were not created just to consume resources, you were put on this earth to make a contribution.'
>
> Mother Teresa

2018–2022 – A SELECTION OF EXTRACTS FROM JOURNAL ENTRIES

Contribution is looked upon as an outwardly action, bestowed on society. The focus is on what we have added and brought to others. It is about what we are leaving behind for future generations. It is about our time on earth and whether this has made a positive difference to society. It is about what mark or set of influences we have left for others to see or perhaps be impacted by. These are indeed interesting thoughts. They may raise sombre questions and be a cause for reflection at this point. We may be stopped in our tracks, which may have been a constant state of doing. Are we just doing activities in the busy mode? Is the activity of doing centred with its impetus from Being or is it all just one bit of craziness with no particular order, no particular sense, no particular intention? Is it just punching in time until our time ceases to be – until our number is called?

Our sense of contribution raises a number of questions for us in the many facets and spheres of our life. What has our life been about over the years of active participation in it?

But now I also think that, besides the outward focus on contribution, there is an important inward focus or, should I say, a focus on us as individuals. With this emphasis, the focus centres on the contribution and building blocks of me and you also, as individuals in each of the phases of life. The question to answer is, has each phase of me added to my life? Have I added with growth and confidence to each stage or phase? Now, this year, am I feeling more whole than I was ten years ago and can I see that there is progress? Do I feel different and happier in myself? Do I feel more in love with myself, am I enjoying more of myself, of my experience as me in my life?

* * *

This subject of contribution, finding purpose and meaning in my life, particularly now that I have reached my 60s and am in the 'Third Act', has been a source of concern for me over the last couple of years. Following a review on contribution and 'legacy' over my life to date, I still felt that there was something else still untapped and needing expression. It seemed to be important that I got a handle on it sooner than later as it was niggling me. Time was beginning to march on.

The niggling thing was that although having clearly articulated my mission and purpose over several years as: 'to grow and evolve myself and use my gifts and talents to the fullest, and in doing so support others in realising their dreams and goals', I still felt that I was not quite hitting the right note and that I was not reaching as many people as I thought I needed to. To some degree I felt lost, something was still missing. I did not feel fulfilled in my 'contribution'. My leadership, management development, and personal effectiveness offerings were still effective and well-received by my clients. What else did I need to do?

Why was I holding so steadfastly to the structure of the unfoldment of my mission and purpose, as it was presenting a struggle? Was I going to reach the end of my life with the feeling of not finding continued expression and not having fully reached my purpose in life?

These questions led me into further searching and over the more recent years I have gotten greater clarity, and the gentle answers have emerged. Maybe the fact that I had held rigidly to the belief in my mission, coupled with my pain of disappointment, was indeed my biggest challenge. To be present to joy is the new message I have received. Living and being in states of joy – doing activities which are joyful to me. By finding and connecting with such activities, these would bring me home to my Self. This presented some challenges as joy had eluded me for some time, as struggle and the hard road had been the path more trodden.

One may well ask, why was it so difficult for me to get to this point? The simple answer is that I had felt contribution had to be lofty: more serious, more substantial.

In reviewing my history I have lived a larger part of my life in a 'doing mode coupled with high standards of achievement', although interspersed with personal development activities of meditation and journaling. The predominant theme of 'doing' seemed to have taken hold, and has reflected in my conditioned thinking that the nature of contribution needed to be sombre. I did 'serious' very well. It was second nature to me. Certainly, I had held this viewpoint for a long time and put in considerable efforts in producing what I thought were programmes and offerings that I believed would benefit peoples' lives.

These offerings were successful for the audiences reached. However, I felt that I had not cast my net wide enough. Also, I felt that the deeper spiritual message could not find an outlet through this offering. These factors were feeding into a somewhat negative belief that I was failing to get my message out to the greater community. Something needed to change as I would otherwise sink into unhealthy states.

Now, I had been thrown this lifeline of hope. Firstly, I needed to halt any potential negative spiral in its tracks. Next, I needed to accept where I was as opposed to fighting with my reality. I knew deep down that my offering and what I had been doing for the last fifteen years had now ended. All my efforts put into my currently existing training and development offerings, as well as the new material, were not working out as I thought they would. The approach that I was taking, viewing it as my legacy to leave something worthwhile that would stand as a contribution, was not going to be as I thought it would be. It was further away from me, and the end game was moving nearer. This notion filled me with fear.

Now, I owed it to myself to stop any potential spiral, to realise my worth and equally to listen more to my inner guidance. The doing mode urgently needed to take a backseat. The solutions from the past were outmoded and I needed to be patient and trust that the answers and guidance would come to me. Armed with this inspiration, I now had the possibility of shaking myself, getting up, dusting myself down and moving forward with greater hope and getting on board with life. My faulty fixation with my declared mission and, more so, the manner of its unfoldment has now been dropped. It has been replaced by the dawning that the purpose of life is to experience it and live a life from joyful states of being, which developed after my struggle. Being unfolds by being fully present to each moment; to have each moment count and lived joyfully. Only from this state can I truly give to others – be a source of joy to others, be a source of love.

Everything passes is something that I remind myself. 'The words 'the depth of our suffering can result in the height of our joy' from the Dalai Lama have landed with me. This came to pass after the realisation that perhaps wanting to be different through seeking more and bigger achievements ends up with us really missing the point of being.

Leonard Cohen is one of my all-time favourite artists and the wonderful lyrics of 'If It Be Your Will' speaks volumes to me.

The struggle I experienced in my life purpose, contribution, and legacy over the last couple of years, together with the personal stresses and working through each of these, led me on a deeper search. This search has been rewarded with growth in all aspects of my life. Having a clearer understanding of contribution and my purpose has led me to a safer, happier and more fulfilling place. Surrender, acceptance, forgiveness, and compassion were qualities speaking out to me over this time and ones which I continue to develop. Making the conscious choice of keeping my heart open is essential to my continued growth. Coupled with this is present moment awareness: no clinging to the past and equally no craving for the future.

My readings have brought me into a deeper, more centred and connected place: in greater alignment with my true essence. In addition to joy being reached through consciously choosing and experiencing activities which are personal sources of joy (outward action-based) there is also the inward focus of developing qualities both mind- and heart-based. Working and continuing to develop these brings deep joy from within. Uncovering the eight pillars of joy – perspective, humility, humour, acceptance, forgiveness, gratitude, compassion and generosity – has brought me into deeper states of connectedness. A number of books mentioned in the References section have brought greater freedom to all aspects of my life. Absorbing the wisdom in my readings and more particularly engaging in practices brings me into greater states of joy and alignment with Source.

'There is a crack in everything. That's how the light gets in.'
Leonard Cohen, *Selected Poems, 1956–1968*

A life lived in the highest states is about living with love and joy. This is the compass heading I set in all my endeavours. A simple question to ask myself several times a day is: am I benefiting from this activity now? So, in asking this question I am probing as to whether the activity is leading me into states of joy and happiness or not. If not, it is not benefiting me; nor is it beneficial to others. My contribution in fact would be a deficit to myself and others. Finding joy by experiencing it and living from this space is my purpose and indeed my contribution.

For it is only from filling ourselves up with love and joy that our gifts to others can be truly valuable. Contribution and legacy will find their way for expression from this state. These are now unfolding in an effortless way as I trust, relax and open into oneness with Source.

Being present to love and joy in all aspects of my life is the resounding message. Connecting into these states each day is essential for me to live from this higher state of being – it is, after all, my true essence. Meditation is the key to gaining access to this deeper connection so that I can bring it forth more fully into my daily life.

For each day is an opportunity to build on the contribution of the previous day. In this way life can evolve. I can work on refining and honing myself, increasingly – becoming wiser, more mature, more understanding of my spiritual nature and my path to deepening my connection with my True Self. This path has been defined in several ways by these different teachings. But what is most important is that I am listening to myself – my True Self. Unlike my previous searching in years gone by, I realise the full import of being true to myself. I'm listening more intensely to what my soul is drawing me towards, listening to that still small voice within. The solution to my challenge has been to listen. Through the busyness of doing, I was keeping myself from not finding my Self – the part of me that is constant, that does not change. The key is practicing and getting to this stillness, peace and quiet while listening and dropping the incessant drive to do. It is only then that I will finally come home to myself and BE.

Perhaps in my rush with doing and the importance I had placed on legacy and my contribution to life, I had missed the essential point about enjoying my life experience. Living my life totally, feeling alive, engaging with life and things that connect me to love and joy. This engagement with life meant that I was more conscious of living in the present. In this way of living, there are no regrets from the past and no longings for the future: this is simply living each moment consciously. The more I practice and am consciously aware of life, the more the theory becomes the practice.

Being present to Now, to reality, opens the space to live to my highest potential. It's important to notice drifting off from this state. With awareness you can gently move back and regain present moment awareness. Acceptance of oneself is a necessary ingredient and the attitude of gratitude is a good running mate. Being willing to shine my light, my True Essence and dropping the motivating force of the Egoic Self brings me to experiencing greater degrees of fulfilment. Allowing the expression of my gifts and talents connects me with my True Essence – and leads to experiencing pure consciousness. Coming into wholeness and wisdom I come into Being more, being my True Self and living authentically from this.

The lasting and ever-enduring aspect in my life has been my connection and continuance with my inner work in reaching greater alignment with my True essence: Source. Now more than ever, I take one step and put it in front of the other. I focus on what gives me joy. I walk Caminos in Northern Spain. I am now more present in the moment of each step of my life. I have a clearer, more focused, yet paradoxically relaxed sense of purpose. I am continuing deepening practices inspired from my readings on joy and living untethered in the present moment. My offerings in the writing projects and training programmes/seminars allow me an outlet to express myself while at the same time adding to my life purpose. My art has and continues to be my anchor into the present moment and states of joy.

> 'Find ecstasy in life; the mere sense of living is joy enough.'
>
> Emily Dickinson

PART IV

Concluding Comments

13

Final Thoughts

In concluding, *Power of W: Women Thriving in Their Third Act* presents my thoughts on how women have immense potential to live a more impactful life, one that is going deeper and developing into wholeness. The 3 Cs were developed as stepping-stones to this expanded life. These keys act as catalysts to living life with passion, power and purpose as you connect and align yourself more with your true nature, your True Self. Living from this Authentic Self, you radiate your true essence into everything you do with the added benefit of the rippling outward effect reaching others.

The three strands – the 3 Cs of Conscious Presence, Connection and, finally, Contribution – can be developed individually and synergies sought. Interweaving these strands, integrating and embedding them deeply into our lives, is a powerful practice. I believe that the 3 Cs present the most significance and greatest impact when we fully engage with them in our Third Act, where they crescendo.

These 3 Cs talk to us women standing in our own space and knowing who we are, Who We Really Are. At the core of our being we are divine beings having a human experience.

The 3 Cs also relate to our connections and community through each of the distinct roles we have in our life. It encompasses how we can influence these for the greater good, adding more depth, richness and meaning to these interactions. It is about how we show up in these interactions, being truly present and conscious. Taking responsibility for our part in each of these interactions can consciously bring the best version of ourselves to each. By always connecting within, we align ourselves with our true nature of love and joy.

Finally, the third strand is about our unique contribution: our gift to the world. We all have something special to contribute. It is important to acknowledge this firstly. Tapping into these gifts, we then find our passion and joy in experiencing and expressing them. Also, we need to be mindful of developing qualities of both mind and heart to living joyfully, mentioned previously within the text. Living from a confident, authentic and centred space, we have the opportunity to share these gifts with others.

Understanding, appreciating and accepting our uniqueness is crucial: really knowing who we truly are. T.S. Elliott's lines from *Four Quartets* about truly knowing ourselves speaks volumes in this regard.

Change is an integral part of growth. We need this to open up to the Divinity within each of us, within every life. John Henry Newman's idea of growth is fitting – to grow is to change and to be perfect is to change often.

All change involves risk. The reward is that we embrace more of our Authentic Self in each day that is presented to us. Connecting deeply within, experiencing and expressing our True nature is our birthright.

It is my hope that the words contained within the covers of this book reach you in a deep way, fanning into flames of passion and awakening as you reconnect with your True Self and shine your uniqueness into the world and live joyfully.

> 'Your task is not to seek for love, but merely to seek and find all the barriers within yourself that you have built against it.'
>
> Rumi

Appendix

The following pages contain information about some different tools and techniques you may find useful on your personal development journey:

- Journalling
- Visualisation
- Affirmation
- Meditation – Going within
- Goal Setting – SMART goals
- Reflection – Borton's model
- Gratitude
- Mindset – Refuting irrational ideas
- Dealing with a traumatic event – SARAH
- Tuning into joy

CAVEAT: These tools and techniques are mentioned in order to provide guidance on tools that may help the reader. Support and counselling from trained professionals should be used where required.

Journaling

Journaling is a self-improvement tool, an active process which connects with your inner being. It should not be confused with keeping a diary.

There are a number of benefits that can be derived from journaling, as one is monitoring one's own internal processes. The process can be beneficial for the integration of psychological parts within oneself that previously have been in conflict. The journaling process can also help in seeing the changing cycles within your life. It connects to the highest aspect of yourself, the source of your essence, creativity and wisdom.

A straightforward way to start this practice is to get an ordinary A4 pad. Create a space in your day to write about any event you deem important. Describe how it affected your emotions, what your thoughts were, your interactions. Also include any realisations that you have gained.

With practice you will gain more insights into your life, how you manage yourself, and what you could do to change and adopt more enabling behaviours. This process makes you more aware and with this awareness you become more conscious of the choices you make.

Journaling is a powerful tool for self-growth.

VISUALISATION

This is a fundamental process in goal achievement. Simply put, it is about imagining very clearly what you want to happen, as if it has already happened. It is about creating an inner experience of what it would be like to have your goal realised. The best way to do this is by closing your eyes. In your mind's eye, paint a picture of the situation, making it as emotionally rich and filled with sensory details as possible, imagining your goals as if they were already true.

Remember to put yourself in this picture.

The key steps are as follows:

Step 1: Select a goal

Example 1: 'I would like to be more open to criticism.'
Example 2: 'I would like to be more flexible in seeking out opportunities to learn.'

Step 2: Construct an affirmation about the goal

State the goal in a simple sentence, in the present tense as if it were already true.

Example 1: 'I am open to criticism, and I willingly accept other people's opinion of me.'
Example 2: 'I actively seek out opportunities to learn.'

Step 3: Picture your goal as if It were already true

Picture the goal by either seeing it in your mind's eye or by feeling it.

Example 1: See someone interacting with you and giving you feedback. See yourself being calm and open to this feedback. Sense that you are okay receiving this feedback and that your body is relaxed while the other person is communicating with you.
Example 2: See yourself starting up a new project that is challenging. Feel excited as you know this will present you with a sense of fulfilment and new learning experiences that you value.

Step 4: Let go of your goal

This means you do not try to make it happen. You just relax and let the creative process within you go to work to produce it. Then go about your daily routine – be sure to follow your intuition and be open to growth and change.

Affirmations

Affirmations expand your beliefs and stimulate your imagination. Affirmations can be developed by using a series of positive present-tense statements about the benefits derived from your goals. Write out short sentences using the points below for guidance and make the sentences as emotionally rich as possible.

When working on a particular aspect, repeat the affirmation at least ten times a day. You can read it out and also recite it. Work with each or several affirmations for a number of days.

The following are points to remember when developing affirmations:

1. Write in the present tense.
2. Write the sentence with positive language.

3. When writing affirmations, be as passionate as possible about it.
4. If some doubts and resistance enter your mind, write these on a separate sheet. They can be dealt with later (See item 6 below).
5. Go back to writing the affirmations to complete the process.
6. Now review the sheet containing your resisting thoughts, which are the barriers preventing you from getting what you want. Develop an affirmation to address these doubts.
7. Keep working on your affirmations daily over a few days by writing them about ten times and also saying them aloud with as much passion and conviction as you can.

Example

Responsibility

- I am the author of my life and I create my reality.
- I act from the position of personal power.
- I have the power to change a situation by choosing more life-affirming and enhancing thoughts.

Meditation – going within

Meditation is a process of focusing the mind on an object or activity. It is an inward focus of attention, concentrating on a repetitive focus such as breathing or a word or prayer. By continuing this for 20 minutes or more, the body and mind begin to quieten down.

In the process of meditation, be aware that the mind is active but with consistent practice you can reduce reactivity to your thoughts. Take on the role of observer or witness to your thoughts, feelings or sensations as they arise and allow them to pass. When you become aware that your mind has wandered, you can choose to gently bring your mind back to your focus word or to your breath. It is beneficial to develop an attitude of acceptance towards whatever happens during the process.

Let us work through an example of a centring meditation. The key elements needed for effective meditation are:

- Place yourself in a quiet environment that is free from distractions. Make sure to take the phone off the hook or turn your mobile off.
- Assume a comfortable position that you can maintain easily for 20 minutes.
- Gently close your eyes.
- Choose a phrase, sound or object to focus on:
  - *Example phrase: 'I am peaceful and calm.'*
  - *Example sound: 'Om' – if necessary, check YouTube for the correct pronunciation of the sound.*
  - *Example object: A golden light focused on your heart centre, or your breath. If you choose your breath, focus on the in-breath while inhaling and on the out-breath as you exhale.*

  Using a phrase, sound or objects helps your focus so that distracting thoughts pass. If you get distracting thoughts, once you become aware of them gently bring your attention back to your focus.
- Continue your focus for 20 minutes or so and when you are ready to come out of meditation, gently open your eyes, come back to the here and now and continue about your day.
- Be as open as you can to whatever the experience brings.
- If you wish, you can write about your thoughts and experiences in your journal.

Goal setting – SMART goals

The acronym of 'SMART' goals has been around for a long time.

S = **S**pecific
M = **M**easurable
A = **A**chievable (and **A**ction-Based)
R = **R**ealistic and **R**elevant
T = **T**imebound

Let us use an example.

Goal: I am going to meditate every day for 20 minutes each day.

Specific: Yes, it is clear as to what needs to be achieved – the frequency and duration are specified.

Measurable: Yes, I could set an alarm for each day to ensure that I remember to meditate.

Yes, I could also set a 20-minute timing alarm for the meditation.

Yes, I can make an entry on a calendar every day once the meditation is completed. I can also check my calendar each month to see whether I achieved my goal for a given month.

Achievable: Yes, this 20-minute meditation is achievable each day.

and Action-Based: I could decide that my meditation practice will occur first thing in the morning at the start of my day so that I get into a routine with meditating.

Realistic (and Relevant): Yes, it is realistic and relevant to my goal of reaching calmer states and practicing meditation regularly.

Timebound: Yes, I have stated 20 minutes per day.

Reflection – Borton's model (1970)

This reflective model is quite simple and often used as the first step on the ladder of the reflective practitioner. This model encompasses three simple questions to be asked of the experience or activity to be reflected on: 'What?', 'So what?' and 'Now what?'

Melanie Jasper endorses the use of this model by novice practitioners and students, as it allows novices to reflect in the 'real world of practice', therefore allowing them to be analytical regarding their developing practice.

What?

This is the description.

Examples: What was the problem? What was my role? What happened? What did I do?

So what?

This is the analysis.

Examples: What was so important about this experience? What did I learn?

Now what?

This is the synthesis.

Examples: Now what do I need to do? Now what might be the consequences of my actions?

Now what do I do to resolve the situation/make it better?

GRATITUDE

Here are a few suggestions to cultivate the healing power of gratitude.

- Make a list of everything for which you are grateful.

  Example: Start with you – your senses, career, education, where you live, etc. Then move on to your relationships and extend from there.
- Before you get out of bed in the morning, can you think of one thing for which you are grateful?
- At the close of each day, reflect on the events of the day and itemise three things that you were grateful for over the course of that day. It is a wonderful way to close each day.

MINDSET – REFUTING IRRATIONAL IDEAS

This section briefly introduces a sample of therapies.

Cognitive therapy is based largely on the work of psychologists Dr Aaron Beck and Dr Donald Meichenbaum, and psychiatrist Dr David D. Burns. This technique can help you work constructively with thoughts, beliefs and attitudes that cause unnecessary stress and problems.

Cognitive therapy recognises that self-defeating thoughts, negative statements, and irrational beliefs adversely affect our mood, behaviour and health.

Cognitive restructuring is one of the techniques used in cognitive therapy. It helps change the way we think. By recognising the negative automatic thoughts and irrational beliefs and their effect on our physical, emotional and behaviour levels, we can choose to change some of these automatic thoughts. These changes in turn change our thoughts, emotions and behaviour.

So, the antidote is to become aware of the automatic thought and identify it. Take a step back before you get sucked into the negative spiral of events associated with automatic thoughts. Breathing is very useful in these situations. By creating this space for yourself you can ask yourself:

- What's going on in the situation?
- Why am I so upset?
- Is it really this bad?
- Does my reaction help?

Reflecting in this way, you can then choose how you wish to respond rather than having a kneejerk reaction with negative automatic thoughts.

Albert Ellis developed Rational Emotive Therapy – a system to address irrational ideas or beliefs and replace them with realistic statements. He postulated that emotions have nothing to do with the actual event. Rather, between the emotion and the event is self-talk, which produces the emotion.

The Beliefs Inventory associated with Rational Emotive Therapy is designed to uncover particular irrational ideas which cause stress. Albert Ellis suggested ten basic irrational ideas:

- It is absolutely necessary for an adult to have love and approval from peers, family and friends.
- You must be unfailingly competent and almost perfect in all you undertake.
- Certain people are evil, wicked, and villainous, and should be punished.
- It is horrible when people and things are not the way you would like them to be.
- External events cause most human misery – people simply react as events trigger their emotions.
- You should feel fear or anxiety about anything that is unknown, uncertain, or potentially dangerous.

- It is easier to avoid than to face life's difficulties and responsibilities.
- You need something other or stronger than yourself to rely on.
- The past has a lot to do with determining the present.
- Happiness can be achieved by inaction, passivity and endless leisure.

Challenging irrational ideas

- Step 1: What are the objective facts of the situation?
- Step 2: Describe your self-talk.
- Step 3: What is your emotional response?
- Step 4: Challenge and change the irrational self-talk. Things to address:
  - Identify the irrational idea
  - Check whether there is any rational support for this idea
  - What evidence is there for the falseness of the idea?
  - Does any evidence exist for the truth of the idea?
  - What is the worst that can happen?
  - What good can happen?
- Step 5: Substitute alternative self-talk.

DEALING WITH A TRAUMATIC EVENT – SARAH

'SARAH' is the acronym which describes the typical states encountered in our emotional response to trauma or bad news. It can be represented as a curve: starting with Shock, dipping down to Anger then reaching the lowest point of the curve at Rejection, before moving upwards into the more positive states of Acceptance and finally Healing.

SHOCK – in relation to the situation or event

ANGER – at the party/parties involved or maybe yourself

REJECTION – Rejection/resentment or resistance/rationalisation: the information is reconciled or explained away; a defensive mechanism comes up ('not my fault')

ACCEPTANCE – of the reality of what is. A surrendering to what is.

HEALING – Having worked through the previous stages, the final stage is healing. Coming to terms with the situation/event and no longer being held back by it. A stage of peace.

Tuning into Joy

An interesting exercise that I learned on my April 2022 Camino was to check whether I was in joyful states each day. Perhaps you will find this exercise below beneficial.

- Set up your alarm to ring every two hours of your waking day.
- When the alarm goes off, stop what you are doing and check in with yourself to see if you are feeling joy. If the answer is yes: great! Otherwise see what you can do to recover joy, or at least the state next available to you to raise your vibration. Then gradually reach for the next higher vibrational state. Ultimately, you have the potential to reach for joyful states.

Try this exercise for a week and see how you feel about it.
Do you want to continue and incorporate this into your daily life?

Qualities to cultivate and develop joy

The Book of Joy mentions eight qualities associated with joy. Below are some thoughts on each.

- Acceptance
  - We need to accept the reality in front of us. This could be painful at times, but it is pointless denying its existence.
  - There is no point in arguing with reality, we cannot escape it.
  - A good question to ask when the situation is unpleasant at least to us is whether you can use the situation to get something positive out of it.
  - Acceptance frees us up to move into joy.

- Compassion
    - Focus on others and their suffering rather than having an inward focus on self.
    - It is important to remember to have Self-Compassion – we sometimes can be too hard on ourselves.
    - Developing compassion takes time. It is said that when you have compassion you have all the other virtues.

- Forgiveness
    - We can set ourselves free by forgiveness of others who have wronged us. Not doing so will result in our pain continuing. In effect we will be imprisoned by the other.
    - Forgiveness does not mean we forget, nor does it mean we accept or approve of the wrongdoing. We can still address the wrongdoing whilst remembering the humanity of the individual/s involved.

- Generosity
    - Our life can really be enhanced when we extend ourselves to make someone else happy.
    - We feel better when we give.
    - It is said that in giving we receive.
    - Generosity is an output of compassion.

- Gratitude
    - Be grateful for the gift of life and to experience life. A good practice is to be grateful every morning and be grateful of the gift of another day.
    - Be grateful for all that we have been given rather that hold the view of what is lacking.
    - Gratitude is a key ingredient to having joy in your life and embracing reality.

- Humour
  - Laughing wholeheartedly is good for us and our health.
  - Laughing has been described as a key to happiness.
  - Laughter and humour are a good antidote to stress.
  - Humour, and particularly being able to laugh at ourselves, is a good quality to develop. It shows our humanity.

- Humility
  - Seeing ourselves as not above anyone self is wise. It is good to remember that we are all one.
  - If we think of ourselves as superior we can end up with isolating ourselves from others.

- Perspective
  - What is our perspective of life?
  - Having the ability to reframe our situation more positively is beneficial. This reduces stress.
  - It is good to stop in a given situation and breath before choosing to react. This creates the space to review the event from a wider perspective.
  - Moving beyond our limited perspective helps us to change the way we see a situation. This in turn will influence our thoughts, feelings and behaviours.
  - We have more choices on how to react when we step back and view things from a wider perspective. We have the freedom of choice.

References

Benson, H. and Stuart, E.M. (1993) *The Wellness Book, The Comprehensive Guide to Maintaining Health and Treating Stress-Related Illness*, New York: Fireside Simon and Schuster.

Borton, T. (1970), *Reach, Touch and Teach: Student Concerns and Process Education*, USA: McGraw-Hill.

Chopra, D. (2009) *Reinventing the Body, Resurrecting the Soul*, New York: Rider.

Chopra, D. and Keys, A. (2021) *21-Day Meditation Experience – Activating the Divine Feminine: The Path to Wholeness, with Alicia Keys and Deepak Chopra*, https://21-daymeditation.com/category/activating-the-divine-feminine/.

Chopra, D. and Winfrey, O. (2021) *Miraculous Relationships with Oprah and Deepak*, https://21-daymeditation.com/category/miraculous-relationships/.

Covey, S. (1992) *The Seven Habits of Highly Effective People*, London: Simon & Schuster.

Covey, S.R., Merrill, A.R. and Merrill, R.R. (1994) *First Things First*, London: Simon and Schuster.

Dali Lama [Tenzin Gyatso] and Tutu, D., with Douglas Abrams (2016) *The Book of Joy: Lasting Happiness in a Changing World*, London: Hutchinson.

Davis, M., Eshelman E.R. and McKay, M. (1995) *The Relaxation and Stress Reduction Workbook*, fourth edition, Oakland, CA: New Harbinger Publications Inc.

Ellis, A. and Greiger R. (1977) *Handbook of Rational Emotive Therapy*, New York: Springer.

Gaffney, M. (2011) *Flourishing: How to Achieve a Deeper Sense of Well-Being, Meaning and Purpose – Even When Facing Adversity*, Dublin: Penguin Ireland.

Goleman, D. (1999) *Working with Emotional Intelligence*, London: Bloomsbury.

Jasper, M. (2003) *Beginning Reflective Practice*, Cheltenham: Nelson Thorn.

Kerrigan, J. (2015) *Old Ways, Old Secrets – Pagan Ireland: Myth * Landscape * Tradition*, Dublin: The O'Brien Press Ltd.

Maslow, A.H. (1943) 'A Theory of Human Motivation', *Psychological Review* 50: 370–396.

McGarry, A. (2017) *CARE of Leadership: A Practice for Developing Leadership Effectiveness*, Dublin: Orpen Press.

Morris, Dermot (2022) Interview on the *Brendan O'Connor Show*, RTE Radio One, 9 October 2022.

Nilan, Judith L. (2015) *A Legacy of Wisdom: The Genius, Power, and Possibility of Ireland's Indigenous Spiritual Heritage*, Home Colony Washington, https://stonefireblog.com/.

O'Donohue, J. (1997) *Anam Cara – Spiritual Wisdom from the Celtic World*, London: Bantam Press.

O'Donohue, J. (2012) *The Four Elements: Reflections on Nature*, Dublin: Transworld Ireland.

Robbins, Tony (n.d.) 'Mind & Meaning: Discover the 6 Human Needs – These Core Needs Drive Every Decision You Make', *The Tony Robbins Blog*, www.tonyrobbins.com/mind-meaning/do-you-need-to-feel-significant/.

Sinek, S. (2009) 'How Great Leaders Inspire Action', *TED*, video online available from: www.ted.com/talks/simon_sinek_how_great_leaders_inspire_action, accessed 20 August 2012.

Singer, M.A. (2007) *The Untethered Soul*, Oakland, CA: New Harbinger Publications and Noetic Books.

Tolle, E. (1999) *The Power of Now: A Guide to Spiritual Enlightenment*, London: Hodder and Stoughton.

Tolle, E. (2002) *Practising the Power of Now: Meditations, Exercises and Core Teachings from The Power of Now*, London: Hodder and Stroughton.

Walsch, N.D. (1997) *Conversations with God: Book One*, London: Hodder and Stoughton.

Both the training programmes and seminars 'REIGNITE: The Retirement Ready Programme' are provided at regular intervals. For further information visit the website www.annmcgarry.com.

To book your place on a programme/seminar or if you wish to avail of one-to-one coaching contact us directly on the following address:

annmcgarry.events@gmail.com

For personal development journeys which may include the above topics contact us at the above email.

For signed paperback books contact us directly on the following email address:

annmcgarry.books@gmail.com

Or by mobile:

00353 87 2771317

We would be delighted to hear from you on how the material in *Power of W: Women Thriving in Their Third Act* has supported you in transitioning into this latest phase in your life.

Join us on Ann McGarry's Facebook community: 'Thrive in Your Third Act'.